C000156446

NORTH NORTHUMBERLAND'S MINOR RAILWAYS:

Volume Three
Sandstone, Whinstone & Gravel Lines

by
Roger Jermy

THE OAKWOOD PRESS

© Oakwood Press & Roger Jermy 2011

British Library Cataloguing in Publication Data
A Record for this book is available from the British Library
ISBN 978 0 85361 705 1

Typeset by Oakwood Graphics.
Repro by PKmediaworks, Cranborne, Dorset.
Printed by Information Press Ltd, Eynsham, Oxford.

> **This book is dedicated to my wife, Diana,**
> **who visited many of these sites with me.**
> **Her patience is, thankfully, almost unlimited.**

From the same author
Northern Northumberland's Minor Railways:
  Volume One: Brickworks, Forestry, Contractors, Military Target railways
  and various other lines (ISBN 978 0 85361 703 7)

Northern Northumberland's Minor Railways:
  Volume Two: Colliery & Associated Lines
  (ISBN 978 0 85361 704 4)

In preparation:
Northern Northumberland's Minor Railways:
  Volume Four: Limestone Industry Lines

Published by The Oakwood Press (Usk), P.O. Box 13, Usk, Mon., NP15 1YS.
E-mail: sales@oakwoodpress.co.uk
Website: www.oakwoodpress.co.uk

Contents

Simplified Geological Map of Northern Northumberland

Key

 CHEVIOT GRANITE

 ANDESITE LAVAS

 CEMENTSTONE GROUP

 FELL SANDSTONE GROUP

 WHIN SILL DOLERITE

 CARBONIFEROUS LIMESTONE AND SCREMERSTON COAL GROUP

Introduction

This book, like the two previous volumes in the series, covers 'minor railways' in the Berwick-upon-Tweed and Alnwick districts. These 'minor railways' include a variety of industrial and small private lines, of a variety of track gauges and with a variety of forms of motive power: locomotives, fixed engines, horses and even manpower. Excluded are lines belonging to the 'main line' companies and those which were operated as sidings from these lines. This volume, for example, excludes the short line leading to Easington Quarry, Belford, as it was always operated as a siding from the main line.

Nevertheless a few liberties have been taken! For example this volume includes the story of the narrow gauge railway linking the Blaxter Quarry in Redesdale with Knowesgate station even though, soon after leaving the quarry, it departs from the Alnwick District.

The lines covered in this book were constructed for obtaining 'hard stone' for a variety of purposes, including stone for buildings, bridges and roads. All were associated with either whinstone or sandstone, except for one which operated in association with the collection of river gravel. Included are certain lines which were 'proposed' but where the actual construction of lines of rails is uncertain. Descriptions of various quarry lines associated with the limestone industry will appear in the final volume of the series.

The text has attempted to place these small railways into their social, geographical and historical context. Hopefully this will widen the readership of the book. The purist may consider it an important omission that lists of source materials and references have not been included after each chapter. If readers wish to make an individual study of the sources that have been consulted then they are cordially invited to get in touch with me via the publisher. Whilst researching for the book it has been considered a top priority that original sources be consulted, and that visits be made to as many of the sites as is practicable or possible. Oral ('anecdotal') evidence, and evidence from secondary sources, such as newspaper reports, has been used on various occasions. However, memories, particularly of events that happened nearly a century ago, may have become clouded, and every effort has been made to find written or photographic material which corroborates the evidence of the spoken word. For example information, passed to the author by word of mouth, has suggested that, some years ago, there was a railway at a quarry at Branxton, north of Wooler. However, visits to the site and searches of documentary records have failed to discover any evidence which might confirm this. With this unconfirmed line, and with the others that appear in this volume I would be delighted to receive further information which will add to the historical record. However, I accept full responsibility for any mistakes appearing in the text.

Throughout I have used the units, whether imperial or metric, which are relevant to the date of operation of each railway. No attempt has been made to convert these units into other forms. Thus boiler pressures, for example, are referred to in 'pounds per square inch' and costs are described in 'pounds, shillings and pence' where the original sources used these. In various places in the text, locomotive builders' names have been abbreviated; a key to these appears towards the end of the book.

Prior permission must *always* be sought from landowners or tenants before visits are attempted to lines which are on private property. Possession of a copy of this volume does not provide a licence to trespass! In certain cases the sites of railways, or former railways described here, can pose considerable danger to visitors, for example from steep cliffs and quarry faces, falling rocks, marshy ground or deep water. If visiting any of the railways by private car, please park considerately, avoiding the blocking of minor roads or gateways.

Finally, written or printed records of some of these railways are sparse or incomplete. On-the-ground evidence has disappeared with the passage of time, and, in the case of many of the lines, there is no one alive today with personal memories to impart. The author would therefore welcome the receipt of any material, perhaps from family histories or albums, which adds to the story of any of the lines. Original photographs or postcards, for which the author has been searching for several years, can provide valuable insight into the working of a line. It would be a pleasure to receive details, via the publisher, of any relevant surviving items.

Roger Jermy
Alnwick, Northumberland
2011

A kite surfer speeds along the channel of the Waren Burn passing the end of the jetty at Budle Bay, the former terminus of Brand's railway from Kitling Hill quarry. In the foreground lies part of the 'zig zag' linking the upper and lower parts of the rail system.   *Author*

Chapter One

The Stone Quarrying Industry in Northern Northumberland

As with the British Isles as a whole the solid geology of Northumberland follows a pattern, with the oldest rocks to be found to the north and west, and the younger rocks towards the south and east. Towards the Scottish border in the north-west the old, hard rocks consist largely of rhyolite and andesite into which was intruded a mass of igneous granitic molten rock which now forms the central part of the Cheviot.

Over the rest of Northumberland the rocks are younger and mainly sedimentary in nature. The cementstone layers, extending from the Tweed to the River Coquet, consist largely of soft shales, sandstones and limestones. The fell sandstones are well cemented and outcrop from Berwick southwards forming the moorland areas of Kyloe, Alnwick, Longframlington, Simonside and Harbottle. The Scremerston coal and carboniferous limestone groups consist of coal measures contained within limestones, shale and some sandstone. This sandstone forms the crags at Rothley, Ottercops Moor and the hills at the sides of the upper Wansbeck Valley to the south of the Alnwick District.

At the end of the Carboniferous era, around 300 million years ago, igneous material forced its way between other layers of rock, and formed the 'Whin Sill'. This hard 'whinstone' forms the Farne Islands and the promontories on which Lindisfarne, Bamburgh and Dunstanburgh castles were constructed. It extends inland from Bamburgh and is also found at Craster and near to Alnwick.

Stone from Northern Northumberland has found a variety of uses both locally and much further afield. Traditionally, local dwellings and farm buildings were made of stone quarried nearby, as were walls between fields. Near to the coast, stone was quarried for the construction of piers and quays, whilst many of the early roads received dressings of crushed stone. Large railway viaducts and bridges were also built with local stone.

With the invention and development of mechanized road transport the need for roadstone increased dramatically to provide hard-wearing road surfaces. Whinstone was particularly favoured for kerbs and setts, and, when crushed, was most suitable both for tarmacadam manufacture and as a top dressing. This was to cause the rapid increase in the number of local quarries in the early years of the 20th century. At this time quarries near to railway lines and ports did extremely well as their products could be moved, in large quantities, to parts of the country lacking indigenous hard stone, such as Kent and East Anglia. Later, quarries near to main roads also expanded and use was even made by the county council of gravel obtained from the terraces of the River Breamish.

The stone from the various sandstone quarries has also been in great demand. The weather-resistant and attractively coloured stones from Doddington, near Wooler in the north of the county, and from Blaxter Quarry in Redesdale, have been much sought after for their fine architectural properties. Stone from these quarries has been taken to Scotland and the south of England and incorporated into fine buildings such as churches, public buildings, large stores, railway stations and viaducts.

Small 'internal' railways or tramways were employed at many of the quarries, transporting the stone from the quarry faces to the plant where the stone was crushed and graded. The stone was then often removed by road, as at Brada or Doddington. However, at some quarries the rail system was extended to take the stone away from the quarry, for example to a main line railway connection or to a convenient port from which the stone could be shipped. Lines of this type, for example linking Embleton Quarry and Christon Bank, or Blaxter Quarry with Knowesgate, were of several miles in length. From Moor Hall Quarry such a railway was laid for the transport of stone for a road widening scheme.

The majority of the quarry railways were of narrow gauge though some, such as at the whinstone quarry at Little Mill or the quarry at Ewesley, had standard gauge lines linking with the national rail system. In the smallest quarries the tubs for transporting the stone were often propelled by hand or hauled by horses. Later, particularly as quarries increased in size and their output soared, powered means of moving the wagons became common. Starting in the 19th century this meant the use of small steam locomotives, or stationary engines with winches which hauled the wagons by cable. Occasionally, as at Doddington or Biddlestone, it was possible for stone to leave the quarry on a tramway with gravity providing the motive force. The stone was then loaded into road vehicles at loading bays at the lower ends of each line. Later either diesel- or petrol-fuelled locomotives were employed at many quarries. These had the great advantage of a reduction in 'preparation' and 'disposal' time, their motors being started with the turn of a switch or a starting handle. Early stone-carrying wagons were often wooden sided but these needed constant repair, with most quarries employing carpenters. Later metal-bodied side tippers became commonly used.

Whilst several of the northern Northumberland quarries described here continue to operate into the early 21st century, none is now employing a rail system. Instead, for example at Howick or Belford, conveyor belts transport the stone from the quarry faces to the crushers and screens. The crushed stone, largely for road use or for making concrete, is transported directly from the storage hoppers to its destination in heavy road lorries. Some quarries retain their tarmac plant. Huge lorries are also used to transport large blocks of architectural stone, often along winding country lanes, from quarries such as Doddington and Blaxter.

This volume describes over 30 quarry railways and tramways of various types. Two lines were described in an earlier volume. The first of these, the Spittal Railway, ran from Hudshead Quarry to Spittal and was constructed for the movement of stone for the building of a stone quay. However, its use for moving stone was short-lived and it was converted for the transport of coal from local collieries. The second line, the craneway at Warkworth Harbour, now part of Amble, was constructed for transporting stone for the construction of the piers, protecting vessels at the coal jetties and staiths. It thus seemed logical to deal with these in the volume devoted to the coal industry.

The limestone industry and the development of its associated quarries, railways and tramways will be dealt with in the final volume of this series.

Chapter Two

The Railways and Cableways of the Wooler and Berwick Districts

Wooler is located at the foot of the Cheviot Hills on the A697 Morpeth to Coldstream road, some 15 miles due south of Berwick-upon-Tweed. Four minor quarry railways were located in this area, one at Doddington, one in the Breamish Valley and two on the outskirts of Wooler itself. One cableway, for the raising of stone from a beach-side quarry, is believed to have existed at Scremerston, south of Berwick.

1 - The Doddington Quarry Railway

Doddington village lies on the B6525 Berwick to Wooler road, some 13 miles south of Berwick and about three miles north of the small town of Wooler. Doddington Quarry (NU006328) lies at the top end of a steep track, to the east of this B-road, just a short distance from the present-day Wooler Golf Club. The area was formerly part of the Tankerville Estate.

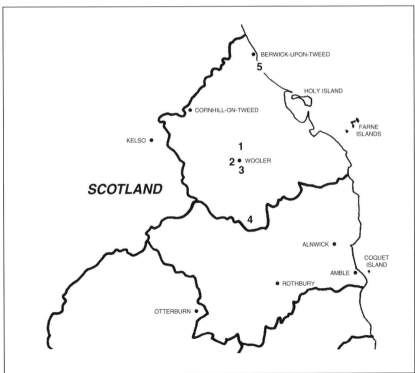

This picture of Doddington Hill was taken from the Berwick Road. The quarry is on the hilltop and the dark diagonal line of vegetation in the centre of the photograph marks the former tramway incline. The modern vehicle track climbs the hillside on the left of the picture.   *Author*

This picture shows the interior of the quarry on Doddington Hill with several large blocks of sandstone awaiting movement away by road. The tramway originally extended into the quarry at this point with 'branches' leading to the left and right.   *Author*

Doddington Hill is made of very good quality sandstone which varies in colour from light golden to dark purplish-pink. It is considered to be a durable stone both for building and paving. In addition to the fine building stone there are also layers of 'bearing', that is poor quality stone, not of sufficiently good quality for building, but suitable for forming a sub-base during the laying of foundations.

Quarrying probably started here in the second half of the 18th century, one Doddington quarryman being identified on the local 1762 'Militia List'. For over 100 years most of the stone was extracted and used by local craftsmen. For example in the 1850s the chapel at the nearby village of Milfield was constructed from Doddington stone, as were some buildings in Wooler. These quarrying activities were, however, on too small a scale to have left much documentary evidence. In the 1881 census, for example, just one local man, Richard Elliott, was described as a quarryman. By the mid-1890s the quarries had increased in size and were operated by a concern known as Messrs Gibb & Sons of Doddington who made a gift, from their profits, towards the restoration of Doddington church. A surviving photograph, believed to date from this time, shows four men at work. However, by 1901 there was just one local quarryman, James Waldie, described as a 'freestone cutter and grocer' in the census. An unusual combination of trades! During this period of time the small quantities of cut stone, mainly for local use, would have been carted down the steep hillside by cart or, perhaps, pack animals along the rough track.

During the 1880s the North Eastern Railway's Alnwick to Cornhill branch railway was being constructed, and Doddington's 'good class' stone was used in several places. For example a little to the north of Mindrum the road between Kilham and Cornhill was carried over the railway by a substantial iron bridge, the abutments for which were built from Doddington stone. Between Wooler and Kirknewton lay Akeld station. The buildings at this station were constructed from 'a pretty stone' obtained from Doddington Quarry. This station, now an impressive private house, with several former railway cottages nearby, is located adjacent to the present A697 road, which the branch formerly crossed by means of a level crossing.

Soon after 1910 the quarry was in the hands of a Newcastle-born, former brick manufacturer from Sunderland, Henry M. Waite, and it is likely that he built the small railway at Doddington to facilitate the transport of the stone from the quarry down the steep hillside to the roadway leading into the village. Here the transfer to road vehicles was effected. North Eastern Railway records for 1913 show that, in that year alone, 3,328 tons of building stone were transferred from road vehicles into rail wagons at Wooler station sidings. This, quite likely, came from Doddington as Yearle Quarry was very small and Scott had not opened his quarry and siding at Wooler by this date (*see later*).

The narrow gauge railway line commenced in the quarry on Doddington Hill. Tracks led from the various quarry faces to the top of the hillside incline; two such 'sidings' appear on the 1926 Ordnance Survey map for example. The rails on these lines could be moved easily as the quarrying moved to new rock faces. The wagons of stone were loaded and pushed, probably by hand, to the top of the incline. Here they were attached to a steel cable running around a

This view looks down the Doddington incline alignment from its half way point. The raised embankment has encouraged the growth of heather, thorn bushes and fine leaved grasses which prefer drier, more stable, conditions compared with the wetter surrounding hillside.   *Author*

The now-disused powder store for the quarry stands on the hillside on the Wooler side of the quarry. Its substantial walls and roof are built with sandstone from the quarry. The remains of its double door lie on the left-hand side near to the doorway. A small raised embankment led to the store from the quarry entrance.   *Author*

large braked drum. The line became a self-acting cableway on an inclined plane. The weight of the descending laden wagons was employed to raise the empty wagons which had earlier discharged their loads at the roadside. Thus, for part of the incline, it was necessary for the rails to be laid in 'double-track' format so that the ascending wagons could pass the descending ones. The brake on the drum ensured that the speed of the wagons was kept under control. The 400 foot contour line is shown on early maps as crossing the mid-point of the incline. No records indicate any accidents or disasters associated with the operation of the line, despite its steep gradient.

The precise period of occupation of the quarry by Waite's concern is not known, but both a lease, dated 1912, and a sale plan, dated 1913, exist in archives. In the 1920s and 1930s about seven men were employed at the quarry. Henry Waite used three steam cranes at Doddington though at some time in the 1940s his son, David, 'inherited' the quarries, employing a Bob Robison (known locally as 'Bunny') as his manager. The quarry railway continued to be operated by Waite's, perhaps irregularly, at least until World War II.

Ken Veitch, a porter-signalman at Wooler signal box between 1935 and 1938, recalls that at this time stone from Doddington Quarry was being shipped by rail from Wooler sidings, mainly to Edinburgh, where it was being used to repair the facings of some of the city's fine buildings. The stone, arriving from the quarry on road lorries, was raised into rail wagons using the station's 5 ton yard crane. This was built in 1885 and had a wooden jib. He remembers that the stone was in blocks of up to 4 tons in weight and that the loading process took a long time as 'the crane inched along in first gear'. Apparently the brake drum of the crane, which was made of metal, was not very effective in wet weather and it was necessary to throw sand onto it to get some grip! The loaded stone wagons were taken away on the 'Tweedmouth Goods' which arrived at Wooler at about 10.30 am and departed northwards on its return journey after the completion of shunting.

For part of the 1950s Messrs Harrisons of Springwell Quarry, Gateshead, operated the quarry and modernized some of the plant. For example the ageing steam compressors were replaced with new ones working on compressed air, thus increasing drilling efficiency eightfold. It has not been possible to discover precisely when Harrisons relinquished their lease. However, some limited quarrying resumed in the 1960s for a just few years, but then, after another period of disuse, a company called Natural Stone Quarries Ltd started to quarry the Doddington stone, though without reinstating the railway. Further stone was removed by road in the 1990s and early 2000s, some once again being used as facing stone for the repair of buildings in Edinburgh such as Edinburgh Castle.

Visits in 2008 and 2009 to inspect the quarry were prevented by barbed wire, with the path into the quarry being barred by a locked gate. A telephone number on a board was provided if further information was required. The quarry appeared to be in the hands of the company called Natural Stone Products Ltd. Geological surveys, conducted in 1997 and 2000 showed that there were still three or four faces available, each three to four metres in depth, with only six metres of overburden needing to be removed.

In 2010 and early 2011 the Stancliffe Stone Co. has been using Doddington Quarry. This concern, 'the UK's largest supplier of natural indigenous dimensional stone' is based at Grange Mill in Matlock, Derbyshire. They advertise the stone as suitable for load-bearing and providing excellent facing stone; their range of products includes pink split face walling and pitch face walling. Within the quarry are numerous huge stone boulders awaiting removal by road. Normally these huge blocks are removed two at a time.

Surveys of the quarry by industrial archaeologists have revealed the remains of an office building, a timber crane and various spoil tips. Outside the quarry on the Wooler side is the former explosives store with very thick stone walls, a metal door and a ventilated wooden door; its roof is still intact though the former lightning conductor has now disappeared. A casual inspection around the outside of the site by the author failed to reveal any lengths of rail still *in situ* or re-employed as fence posts or suchlike. Presumably the wagons and rail were sold for reuse, or for scrap, when the line ceased to operate.

With permission it is possible to park in the car park of the neighbouring Wooler Golf Club and inspect the remains of the incline. It is easily recognized as its partial covering of dry soil tolerant heather makes it stand out from the rather marshy reed- and grass-covered land at its sides. At its upper end it is raised upon a low embankment, partly to even out the gradient and partly to raise it above the wet ground near a small spring. Lower down the line runs, in part, in a very shallow cutting. At its lower end there is a hollow in the surrounding land which may have been the site of a loading bay for road vehicles. Various lumps of stone are found at the sides and lower end of the incline. So far no photographs of the line in operation have been discovered though a couple of photographs have survived showing workmen in the quarry and part of one of the cranes.

2 - *The Scott's Quarry Railway at Wooler*

Scott's Quarry (NT983278) was opened in the early 1920s on Common Road (formerly Common Burn Road), Wooler. This road leads from the direction of the town centre towards the part of Wooler Common between Kenterdale Hill and Brown's Law. It was created on the opposite side of the Humbleton Burn to the ancient earthwork known as Green Castle.

Edward Scott had combined the occupations of motor engineer and quarry owner and it is possible that he started his career as a cycle maker. His quarry first appeared on the Ordnance Survey maps published in the early 1920s.

This small whinstone quarry, and its associated railways, was opened by Scott as a source of rough stone and tarmacadam for road construction and repair. Scott installed a system of elevators, crushers and screens, together with a narrow gauge railway in two parts. The first part was inside the quarry and took stone, in small hopper wagons, from the quarry face to the elevators for feeding into the crushers. The second part was located so that crushed stone could be taken from the screens to a roadside loading bay and the waiting road vehicles. The gauge of the line was narrow, probably of 2 ft gauge, and several small metal-bodied V-tipper wagons were employed. Manpower was used to move the wagons. A tarmacadam plant was also located at the site.

Scott was one of the suppliers of roadstone to Northumberland County Council. Perhaps the earliest surviving record of this appears in the Minutes of the council's Roads & Bridges Committee of 25th May, 1925 when Scott tendered successfully for the supply of 2,000 tons of stone (at 4s.1d. per ton, total £400) for the improvement of the Morpeth to Coldstream road (now the A697). On 27th July of the same year he had success in tendering for the supply of 1,200 tons of tarred stone for the Berwick and Cornhill road (now the A698). Other roads for which Scott supplied chippings were those between Alnwick and Eglingham, and Norham and Shoreswood. For some of these contracts county council lorries were loaded at Scott's Quarry. After the closure of the county council's own Moor House Quarry, near Whittingham, in 1928, Scott became one of the principal suppliers of tarred and rough stone for the improvement of the Morpeth to Coldstream road to the north of Shawdon Hill, 1,000 tons being supplied by 23rd June, 1928, for example. During the years 1925 to 1930 he delivered many more consignments of tarred chippings for the county council, some by road direct to the site of use, others by rail from Wooler station to local stations for transfer to county council vehicles.

Occasionally Scott had difficulty in fulfilling his contracts. For example in 1929 he had contracted to supply 230 tons per day for the Berwick to Cornhill road and the Alnwick road at Eglingham. Because of the limitations imposed by the plant at his quarry he could only manage to deliver between 120 and 130 tons per day. The deficit was made up by the county council turning to McLaren's at Crag Mill Quarry, Belford, and Appleby's of Embleton Quarry. They delivered the extra stone to Norham and Coldstream stations respectively.

Scott possessed at least one steam wagon of his own for use on public roads. The known vehicle was built in 1919 by Clayton & Shuttleworth at Lincoln. It was a 5 ton compound engine and was bought by Scott's in 1928, registration number FE 340. It was bought second-hand from Gapshields Colliery Ltd, at Byron Colliery, Greenhead. This was kept busy both making local deliveries to customers and taking stone from the quarry to Scott's siding on the LNER (formerly North Eastern Railway) branch from Alnwick to Cornhill-on-Tweed. Scott had been delivering stone before this date, the earliest traced records relating to May 1925, so it is likely that Scott owned other vehicles as well. Further evidence that Scott owned, or planned to own, other road vehicles arises from his having tendered for the leading of stone from the Breamish Gravel Depot at Powburn to the nearby Hedgeley station (also on the Alnwick to Cornhill line).

Scott's private railway siding at Wooler was built as a result of an agreement, dated 3rd December, 1926 between Scott and the LNER, represented by George Davidson, the divisional manager for the north-east area of the LNER. 'Scotts Siding' was located close to the level crossing on the Wooler to Berwick road. The Wooler South signal box was located to the north-west side of this crossing. The Plan for the works, drawn up by Delittle, Fenwick & Co. of York, shows that the turnout from the branch line, and the first part of the siding, were to be built by the LNER (albeit at Scott's expense) but that the rest of the siding was to be built by Scott. A loading dock was constructed at the side of the line. Scott

Scott's Quarry was photographed in the early years of the 20th century. The picture shows some of the plant including the crushers and steam boilers. It captures the moment when a steam lorry is loaded from a side-tipper whilst other tipping wagons await their turn to be unloaded.

Berwick upon Tweed Record Office

Scott's steam lorries took much of the stone from his quarry down to the exchange siding on the Alnwick to Cornhill railway close to Wooler station. The branch goods train then took away the stone, often to station destinations within the county, for collection by the County Council, for whom Scott was a major contractor to supply roadstone.   *Collection of Miss Vera Mallon*

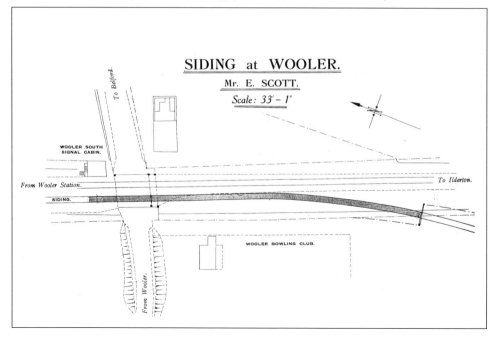

SIDING at WOOLER.

Mr. E. SCOTT.

Scale: 33' = 1"

was to pay the LNER £1 per year in half-yearly payments in addition to the costs of moving goods. The rates were drawn up to include charges for coke, patent fuel, limestone and iron ore in addition to stone! Wagons were delivered to, and picked up from the siding by the branch 'pick-up' goods train. Between 1926 and 1930 Scott delivered much macadam by this route from Wooler to Norham and Coldstream stations for Northumberland County Council road improvements, and gravel to a variety of other rail destinations.

Scott's enterprise is believed to have closed in the late 1930s, close to the start of World War II, as the supply of stone on the cramped site ran out. The railway materials and plant were sold or scrapped and eventually the site became occupied by Redpaths, the local scrap dealers. Fortunately one photograph has been traced showing some of the plant, rail wagons, a steam lorry, and the boilers providing steam for powering the site's equipment.

3 - McLaren's Railway at Yearle Quarry

Yearle Quarry (NT987269), sometimes referred to as Earle Quarry, lies just off the minor road linking Wooler with the hamlets of Earle and North Middleton. Its name has not appeared on Ordnance Survey maps. This road is a continuation of The Brae and Cheviot Street leading from Wooler centre. A broad track, surfaced with stone and gravel, links this minor road with the quarry. The track, which is barred to vehicular traffic by a locked double gate, is about 120 metres long. Pedestrian access to the track, marked as a public footpath by a signpost, is via a side gate. The track leads past the quarry entrance gate which is itself now gated and padlocked. It continues for a short distance beyond the quarry gates to the site of the original loading point for road lorries, before becoming a footpath suitable for walkers only. It continues to Pin Well and Waud House.

The quarry first appeared on the Ordnance Survey maps which were surveyed and published in the 1890s. It was then very small and the quarried stone was used locally. It was not until the 1930s that the locally well-known quarrying firm of McLaren's took over the quarry and stone was removed on a commercial scale. (McLaren's had, for example, operated the large quarry at Crag Mill, Belford, adjacent to the Great North Road, the A1, from the 1920s.) As no further local surveys were carried out there was no update to the OS maps of this area in the 1930s and 1940s. Hence the progress and extent of McLaren's quarrying was not revealed cartographically until after the post-World War II survey.

The OS maps, published in the early 1950s, indicate that the quarry had become considerably enlarged over the previous 50 years. The quarry had two 'buildings', one of which appeared to be the terminus of the small railway, marked as a single line running from the quarry face on the north side of the quarry. No sidings were indicated on the maps; however observers have reported that a small 'fan' of tracks led to various parts of the quarry face when it was in use. Presumably the 'building' at the south end of the railway could have been the crushers and screens. The purpose of the other smaller building

Right: This photograph, taken in the very early 1950s is the only picture discovered that shows the rails in Yearle quarry. A group of children, including a young Alan Holmes, are playing on the remains of a side-tipping wagon. The quarry had been out of use for some years at this time.

Alan Holmes Collection

Below: In the latter half of 2009 Yearle quarry was host to a large Powergrid portable stone screening machine which appeared to have received some recent use, presumably in connection with producing gravel for use on the trackways of the Lilburn Estates.

Author

is not known though its proximity to the quarry faces surely indicates that it was *not* the powder store! Its position at the end of the entrance track may indicate that it was the quarry office or facilities for the quarrymen.

Ironically McLaren's had finished working the quarry around the time that the map was published and the railway had been closed. A visitor in the early 1950s recalled that the facilities in the quarry appeared to be derelict. Despite this, in the absence of further local surveys, the OS maps published in the 1960s and 1970s continued to show the railway and the quarry buildings. More recent maps have marked the quarry as 'Disused'.

Documentation relating to the operation of Yearle Quarry appears not to have survived and the surviving members of the McLaren family cannot add to the story. However it may be the case that Yearle Quarry took over as a local source of stone when the supply from Scott's Quarry, also in Wooler, was discontinued in the 1930s. At this time McLaren's continued to supply the county council with roadstone for use in the most northerly parts of Northumberland and it is likely that Yearle Quarry supplemented the stone obtained from Crag Mill and elsewhere.

Of the railway little is known apart from the evidence obtained from a single photograph taken after closure of the line which shows that the gauge was of about 2 ft and that the lightweight track was spiked to wooden sleepers. Small 'side-tippers' were employed. The chassis of one of these was still in the quarry in 1952. Though McLaren's used locomotives elsewhere there is no record of a locomotive being used at Yearle. In any case the distance between the quarry faces and the crushers and screens was very short and the tippers were probably manhandled over the almost level ground. The crushed and graded stone was removed by road. A concrete-supported loading dock was located on the track a few yards beyond the quarry entrance. Some remains of this have survived to the present.

Today the quarry is in the hands of the Lilburn Estates and Farm Partnership, based at nearby Middleton Hall. This concern purchased the quarry, and the surrounding farm, from the Dodds family of farmers in June 1998. There is no public access to the Yearle site and several warning notices are posted. A fading notice attached to the fence at the side of the quarry gate refers to the site being 'part of a local heritage project'. A large man-made bank prevents a direct view into the quarry from the adjacent public footpath. However, a branch of this path climbs the hillside towards the south shortly after a gate located some 50 yards beyond the quarry entrance. From this vantage point a view into the quarry, perhaps better obtained with binoculars, can be gained. It would appear that the quarry has a continuing, if limited, use as a store for stone. There are large piles of stone in several places though their varied colour (including the red colour typical of Harden Quarry stone from Coquetdale) would seem to indicate that not all of the stone, if any, comes from the adjacent quarry faces. One large item of quarrying plant was located inside the quarry in 2009 and 2010, namely a screening machine identified with the 'POWERGRID' logo. (This portable screening equipment is marketed worldwide by the Terex Corporation.) A pile of rubble nearby appears to be the remains of a concrete and brick building. Pieces of old timber, possibly the remains of railway sleepers lie around and two large diameter concrete pipes are present close to the quarry entrance.

The alignment of the Breamish Valley Railway along the man-made ledge on the side of 'Brough Law' can be seen very easily from the vantage point of the new Peggy Bell's bridge. Much of the hillside consists of screes. *Author*

Evidence suggests that a siding, leading to a loading point at the base of the scree on the left, existed at this point on the railway. The main route of the railway continues along the hillside towards other screes. *Author*

The suggestion that the quarry is in only limited use arises from observations made during visits in 2010 to the adjacent footpath when a pair of buzzards were observed wheeling round over the quarry and a sparrowhawk flew at great speed over the bank from the quarry to harass some great tits in the nearby copse. Apparently red squirrels can also be seen nearby. Despite its proximity to Wooler and the road, this is now a very quiet location!

4 - The Breamish Valley Railway at Ingram

A short-lived World War II mineral railway, located at Ingram, was christened the 'Breamish Valley Railway' by local residents. The River Breamish drains part of the Cheviot Hills. Ingram is a small hamlet located on a minor road about 2½ miles to the west of what is now the A697 leading from Morpeth to Wooler and Coldstream. This narrow minor road commences a short distance to the north of Hedgeley, some seven miles south of Wooler and just within the Berwick District. It parallels the river which is prone to severe flooding after periods of rainfall and must be followed with care. Farm animals roam freely over the road and its surroundings. The railway's former trackbed (NT996164) is located on the land of Lord John, the brother of the current Duke of Northumberland.

The railway served several exposed scree slopes, which furnished stone used for the building, by construction firm George Wimpey, of the local World War II RAF airfields at Boulmer, Eshott (Felton), and Milfield. All three airfields possessed three interlinked runways. The railway was in operation from some time in 1941 until approximately March 1943.

RAF Boulmer, located near the coast to the east of Alnwick, was opened in 1940 as a decoy station for the operational airfield at Acklington a few miles to the south. It originally consisted of grass runways with wooden models of 'Hurricane' fighter aircraft. It became an operational airfield in March 1943 to house the advanced flights of the RAF's 57 Operational Training Unit (OTU); it functioned as a satellite field for Eshott. Later it was the home of No. 9 Battle Training School. To house these units it was necessary to construct 8 in. thick concrete runways and buildings. This was carried out by Wimpey's, the contract being worth £363,000.

RAF Eshott (Felton), located immediately to the east of the A1 road approximately halfway between Alnwick and Morpeth, was under construction by George Wimpey at the same time as RAF Boulmer, being completed in November 1942. Wimpey's contract here involved the construction of both the runways and buildings, as at Boulmer. It was the home of 57 OTU's 'Spitfire' aircraft. The construction contract was worth £534,000.

These two RAF airfields were the only two built by George Wimpey in Northumberland, though they built over 90 elsewhere. Since the end of the war Boulmer has been an RAF Group Control Centre, later becoming involved in the UK's air defences housing the School of Fighter Control. It has a NATO role and also houses the helicopters of 202 'Search and Rescue' Squadron. Eshott is currently owned and operated by Eshott Airfield Ltd, and it is used for small aircraft and microlite flights. Parts of both Eshott and Boulmer airfields have been returned to agriculture.

RAF Millfield was located adjacent to the A697 road to the north of Wooler near to the village of Milfield (note the difference in spellings). Its construction started in August 1941 and it was opened in August 1942. Although planned as a base for bomber aircraft it initially hosted 59 Operational Squadron Training Unit using 'Hurricane' fighters, and, from 1944, units of the United States Air Force who used 'Thunderbolts', 'Mustang' and 'Lightning' aircraft. The contractor involved in runway construction is believed to have been from Sunderland; some 1,000,000 tons of concrete was used in its construction. Today the Borders Gliding Club uses part of the site.

Approximately halfway between Ingram and the end of the public road at Hartside is a narrow road bridge over the River Breamish known as Peggy Bell's bridge. This bridge has recently been rebuilt after the previous one suffered from the effects of severe flooding in the valley. To the south of this bridge lies a hill called Brough Law, the flanks of which are largely formed of screes of loose rhyolite, individual stones varying between about 1 inch and 1 foot in diameter. These screes are known as the 'Glidders' because they are reputed to 'glidder' or glitter when wet. However most of the stones today are covered with lichen making their surfaces dull! It was the 'Glidders' that supplied the stone transported along the Breamish Valley Railway. The railway was about 300 yards in length and ran south-west to north-east along an embankment or ledge, closely following the 500 ft contour. Much of the trackbed of the line appears to have been up to 9 ft in width and the track gauge is remembered as 'two-foot', the same as that employed at the Powburn Gravel Works a few miles distant. The stone was shovelled into 'rail tubs' (actually side tipping wagons) which were manhandled along the line towards the road where there was a loading area. Here the wagons of stone were run onto 'the gantry' from which stone was tipped from the side-tippers directly into George Wimpey's 5 ton lorries for transport out of the valley. The work was carried out on weekdays only, no stone being taken out on Saturdays or Sundays.

The former trackbed can be accessed on foot via a sloping ramp leading from the roadside immediately to the east of Peggy Bell's bridge. At the top of the ramp, and turning to the left, one can see the former loading bay which consists of a 'cut' into the hillside with its walls lined with stone. The loading bay could accommodate just one 5 ton road vehicle. The rails on the tipping gantry were about 10 ft above the road surface in the loading bay. Today the bay houses a thriving colony of ferns. In summer these make photography difficult. However, in winter the aerial parts die back and reveal the crumbling stone facings of the loading bay. (A rough track, not connected with the railway, extends eastwards from this point towards another scree slope. This was the source of much stone used during the construction of the Alnhammoor to High Bleakhope road (in the upper valley of the Breamish) in the early 1950s. A small bulldozer was used to push the loose stone towards the lorry loading bay.)

Returning to the top of the approach ramp it is possible to walk the full length of the line. On the left, almost immediately beyond the top of the access ramp, there is a triangular area which was the site of sidings for the temporary storage of loaded tubs awaiting the arrival of a road lorry, and for empties awaiting return to the screes. The trackbed then proceeds along a ledge, with a man-made embankment on its river or right-hand side, towards other scree slopes where it widens from about 9 ft to some 15 ft. The grassy areas to the left indicate that loading sidings almost certainly existed here. The line then rises very slightly towards its terminus at a large area of scree. Vegetation is beginning to encroach upon the alignment at this point. However, the passage of sheep keeps the route open! The outer edge of the embankment is faced with medium-sized stones and very large stones appear to have been placed at intervals.

The line closed in 1943. However, some local residents recall the line of 'metal tracks' being in place for a short time afterwards. Memories dating from 1949 suggest that all of the rails had been lifted 'well before that year'. Recent Ordnance Survey maps indicate, as an unfenced track, the route of this short-lived railway running beneath the 'Ingram Glidders'.

The new Peggy Bell's bridge (originally built in 1907-08) has been commissioned now that major works, which involved some realignment and repair of the valley road, have taken place. A Bailey Bridge was temporarily used to replace the old bridge whilst the new one was under construction. Much heavy plant was employed at the site and several temporary buildings were erected for the county council's workforce. It is now possible, once again, to park at the side of the road near to the site of the loading bay. There is some off-road parking on the grassy 'haugh' by the side of the River Breamish shortly before the bridge but the ground surface can become very soft after rain.

The loading bay, at which the small tipper wagons discharged their load into road lorries, survives at the side of the Ingram Valley road close to Peggy Bell's bridge. It is easily recognised in winter and early spring before the re-growth of bracken and other vegetation which occurs later in the year.   *Author*

5 - *The Scremerston Gravel Works Cableway*

The last of the lines to be described in this 'miscellany' was an overhead cableway rather than a railway. It was, according to information handed-down orally, operational on the coast to the north and west of Scremerston Mill and Seahouse (NU023497). These buildings are located to the east of the former Scremerston station. The early 1920s editions of the Ordnance Survey maps show what is probably the line of the cableway, linking the beach and the nearby clifftop, very close to the long-disused Cargies Kiln. Map measurements indicate its length as just over 50 yards. Some buildings were indicated at the line's upper end, one being directly opposite the end of the 'line'. This was suggested as a stone crusher. Another building stood nearby and may have been an office or shelter for the workmen. Orally handed-down evidence suggests that stones were brought up from the beach in small 'buckets' before being crushed into gravel. The gravel was then transported in horse-drawn carts for a short distance before being loaded into rail wagons at the siding (formerly the lime siding) at Scremerston station. The possible line of the cableway is shown on a subsequent ordnance map though this repeats the details shown on its predecessor; no additions or alterations were made to the map in the 20 years or so between their publication dates. It is believed that the line was short-lived, having closed by the early 1930s. Documentary evidence identifying the name of the concern obtaining the gravel has not been discovered, though the Carr family, involved with the earlier lime works, may have been involved.

This pantiled cottage, located some 150 metres from both the stone crushers and the jetty, is reputed to have been the site of Brand's offices whilst quarrying was taking place at Kitling Hill between early 1911 and 1914.   *Author*

Chapter Three

The Quarry Lines around Bamburgh and Belford

All of the quarry railways described in this chapter were located in the Rural District of Belford within the Berwick Council District. Four were found to the east of the area, near to Bamburgh or Budle. The remaining two lines were located near to Belford, close to the A1 road. All six were narrow gauge lines and served whinstone (or in the case of Brownieside, sandstone) quarries.

In the first part of the 19th century the Budle Estate had been owned by Earl Grey. The Grey Archive contains papers relating to the exploitation of the whinstone quarry at Budle. Included is an 1828 report from John Dodds concerning this quarry, and the quay and harbour at Budle. This is the earliest record discovered that relates to the quarrying of whinstone in the locality; it involved the possible creation of a railway to link the quarry and quay. The quarry, then entitled 'Budle New Town Quarry', was opened and operated for a few years with some stone being shipped to the south of England (*see Chapter Nine*).

The 'Budle Whinstone Quarries' were later the subject of a lease to Robert Gillow for 20 years, the parchment deed being dated 28th October, 1853. No further evidence has been discovered regarding the extent of his quarrying activities.

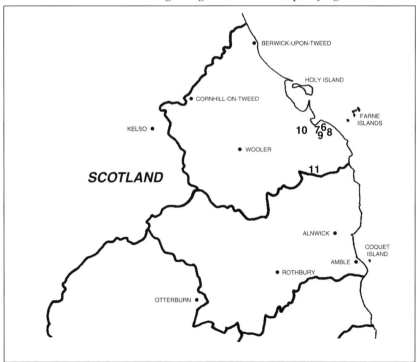

25

In the mid-19th century a certain George Turnbull had rented the Budle Estate from Earl Gray, his lease being due to expire in 1874. However, on the 17th March, 1870, the *Newcastle Daily Journal* reported 'the Great Sale of Northumbrian Estates' at an auction in London. The sale prospectus included the following: 'there are on this Estate, great quantities of whinstone, in some places rising to the surface, easily worked and suitable for pavement and road metal' including 'an old quarry at Galliheugh Bank'. This confirms that the quality of stone was recognized long before the rapid development of the quarrying industry at Bamburgh and Budle which occurred in the early years of the 20th century. The estate, which included 645 acres of fine arable land suitable for barley and wheat, as well the whinstone quarries, was purchased by the Cruddas family of Haughton Castle, for the sum of £37,000.

It was around this time that John Richardson of Little Mill, perhaps acting as an agent for the estate owners, arranged for a certain Mr Scott of Embleton to start quarrying whinstone at Bamburgh. He was to pay 4*d.* per ton for rubble stones, and 4*s.* 6*d.* per ton for winning and dressing 'pavers' (paviours or pavement slabs). An additional 2*d.* per ton was to be paid for loading the above into ships.

These small concerns were to prove the forerunners of later enterprises operated on a very much larger scale.

6 - Brand's Railway at Bamburgh

Two of the railways which operated near Bamburgh were built as a result of the interest of Scottish companies in the whinstone of the area. The first of these companies traded as Messrs Brand & Son of Glasgow. James Brand, who founded the company, was born in 1832 at Montrose. By 1881 he was described as a 'Contractor for Public Works'. He had a large family. Charles, his eldest son, was born in 1868 at Creich in Sutherland. On the death of James he inherited the interests and goodwill of his father's company and traded under his own name. Amongst numerous civil engineering contracts, Charles' company was, for example, involved in the completion of the Aviemore to Inverness line for the Highland Railway in Scotland. Taking over when the previous contractors, Mackay & Mackay, became bankrupt in 1894, Brand completed the line which was opened in November 1898. The works involved the operation of several sandstone quarries.

It was in mid-1910 that the Bamburgh Golf Club, themselves lessees, were informed that the landowner, Mr Cruddas, had let the mining rights, adjacent to their golf course, to 'Charles Brand Ltd, Mining Contractor'. There was much consternation that a railway was planned to be laid across the course! The club Secretary met with Mr Knaggs, the local Manager from the quarry company on 21st December, 1910. Knaggs presented the Secretary with a statement which was worded as follows (as recorded in the Golf Club's Minute Book):

> The Quarry is to be at Kitling Hill.
> The line of tramway will start from there and cross the course towards the west of the Ladies number three tee and will then curve round and follow the bank near its edge to

the seaward of number three green and slope down well below number five green to the Pier at Budle. Blasting will only be required once in several days or perhaps a week and will always be done before 9.00 am. The Men's huts will be at the pier end, with a bothy at the Quarry somewhere near Hutchinson's field wall for the men to feed and shelter in. By terms of this lease the men are not allowed to trespass on the Course and when going to and coming from work are to keep to the right of way, and are not allowed to keep dogs.

Mr Knaggs states that he will do his best to interfere as little as possible with the interests of the Golf Club, and will be willing to meet the Golf Club Committee, if that body should wish to interview him with reference to the Quarry, or the work connected with it, so far as it applies to the course.

Brand's had agreed with the Cruddas Estate to lease the quarry (NY 168353) for a rent of £150 per annum with 6*d.* per ton being paid for each ton of stone removed. It was estimated that the total income to the Estate could be upwards of £600 per annum. The golf course had been paying a rent of just £25 per annum, but offered to increase this to £125 if it would prevent the quarry being leased. Not surprisingly Cruddas declined this offer and the quarrying went ahead.

The quarries were officially commissioned in January 1911. At the time it was stated that as much as 1,200 tons of stone were to be shipped each week. This would require the movement of about 600 wagonloads per week using 2 ton capacity railway wagons.

It was the *Berwick Advertiser* of 30th January, 1911 which first reported to the general public the interest of Brand's (and also Brunton's, *see later*) in quarrying for stone in the area, the same article being carried by the Alnwick newspaper on the following day. It read as follows:

BAMBURGH WHINSTONE

A new era is opening for Bamburgh and its neighbourhood. The country adjacent to the historic village is rich in whinstone of a particularly good quality. Local highway surveyors have known this for a very long time and road metal from quarries thereaway has been in great demand for years. But now it has been 'discovered' by outsiders and arrangements have already been made for having it worked on an extensive scale.

Two Scotch [*sic*] firms are in the field, Messrs. Brand and Messrs. Brunton. The former are opening up a quarry on the Budle Hill, not far from the shore, and a very short line of tramway will enable them to put this stone on board at Budle Quay at practically no cost for haulage. Messrs Brunton have purchased part of the Spindlestone Estate and Waren Estate containing a large area of stone and their output will be shipped to Waren Mill where, in former days, a considerable coastal trade was done in corn and manure.

A few months will see effected wonderful change in this 'corner of the North'. Instead of half a dozen fishing cobles resting on the mud at the mouth of Waren Burn a fleet of boats will invade the bay at every turn of the tide to carry away to southern ports the produce of a great industry. The quietness of the wide expanse of foreshore, hardly now disturbed by the cry of a seabird, will be pierced by the sound of the siren and broken by the roar of blasting powder; and the Laidley Worm of Spindlestone will have its privacy invaded. But legends must go by the board when employment is at stake and there is no doubt that work will be provided for many men by the operations projected.

Six hundred hands is the estimated number that only one of the firms in question will ultimately employ and it will require little stretch of the imagination to see well on to that number engaged in quarrying and dressing and hauling. That time is not just yet but it looms in the future.

Brand's moved quickly despite the problems associated with the leased land being in the middle of the Bamburgh Golf Course. On the 27th January, 1911 the same Berwick paper indicated that preparations for quarrying the whinstone were already in hand:

Machinery is now being delivered daily and a five ton steam crane is now in the works. A huge stone crusher and other up-to-date machinery will be lodged within a few yards of the pier. Over thirty men are at present employed and Mr Knaggs, manager, anticipates having over one hundred men employed in about a couple of month's time. A light railway is now being laid to the old Waren Quay which will be strengthened and where every facility for the loading of vessels will be provided. The stone will be blasted from the crag and thence by rail to the pier where it will be prepared for the different purposes and then be able to load vessels up to almost one thousand tons capacity.

Two powder houses were constructed to store the blasting powder. One was located near to the quarry, the other being of brick construction near the fifth fairway. Other buildings reported to have existed at the quarry included a small engine shed, a workshop and stores. Other documentation reveals that two stone crushers were to be employed near the jetty, both built by Baxters of Leeds. These were to be powered by a steam engine. The five ton crane, originally brought in for use at 'Budle Quay', was built by Thomas Smith & Sons of Leeds. (Later an additional crane was to be used on the quay.) A portable steam engine, by Forster of Lincoln, was obtained to work the crushers. New hoppers for the crushed stone were also obtained. These are believed to have arrived by rail and road. The machinery is said to have arrived in 'new' condition. Its value was stated to have been £10,000.

Meanwhile Belford Rural District Council was concerned about the effect of the railway on some local rights of way, including one allowing public access to Budle Bay. Mr Knaggs, Brand's Manager, had met with the council's surveyor on 24th January at Budle Pier near Heather House. Knaggs proposed that Brand's should raise the public track at this point to facilitate the laying of the railway over it. In addition a new road would be constructed in place of a portion of this same right of way. The surveyor pointed out that it was necessary to maintain access to this part of the shore in case the lifeboat required it. The new road would have to be 'more suitable for the purpose than the existing right of way'. Brand's formally requested permission for these works at a subsequent meeting of the council. This was granted and an agreement was drawn up containing several clauses as regards public indemnity and other matters connected with safety.

The *Alnwick Gazette* of 11th February, 1911 reported that they had already cut the 'tramline' near to the fourth green. The same article suggested that the stone, carried along the line, would be shipped from the old pier at Budle Bay to the Firth of Forth, probably with a view to supplying stone for the building of the Government's naval works at Rosyth.

The first steamer to dock at the old jetty was the *Kestrel* in early March 1911. This vessel was safely brought to its mooring by a local pilot, either Captain Frater or Captain Ferns according to different reports. This vessel brought supplies of coal, timber, tubes and cement for Messrs Brand. Not surprisingly its arrival caused great interest as only the very oldest of the local inhabitants could recall vessels using the jetty!

The same month it was reported that the district council wanted some rough stone from the quarry for the inmates of the local workhouse to break by hand!

The golf club Minutes record that the quarry, and presumably the railway, were in operation by 20th May, 1911. Concern was still being expressed at the club's committee meetings at the impact of the operations on the playing of golf. In April 1911 the Secretary, Mr Stopford, had offered some assurances. No greens on the course were interfered with. The tramway, which crossed the fairway between the third and 17th holes, would merely form a hazard and no golfer would be penalized with his tee shot when playing these holes. Discontent clearly persisted for on 20th May the Secretary said that intending visitors to the course should not pay attention to the rumours that were being circulated. However, the concerns and fears were not groundless as one member, Major General Adye, was nearly killed when a 7 lb. lump of granite was hurled towards a group of players on the second green after an unannounced blasting at the quarry! A similar incident had happened when a group of ladies were playing. Complaints to the rural district council resulted in Brands being required to hoist a flag five minutes before firing. Notices to that effect must be posted in conspicuous places near the quarry. Two horns must be blown, one in each direction, before firing and in addition the quarrymen were to scatter about and warn people in the vicinity!

The quarry and line of rails continued to have an impact on the course. In April 1912 a new rule was introduced to the effect that tee or second shots, lying within two club lengths of the tramway or stones adjoining, could be lifted and dropped on penalty of one stroke. Also, with reference to the 17th hole, '… if the tee shot falls within twenty yards of wagons standing on the tramline in direct line with the hole, the ball may be lifted and dropped to one side of the trucks but not nearer to the hole'. By October of the same year further changes to the course were necessary when the location of the sixth hole had to be abandoned because of 'the dust and nuisance from the stone crushing', and the 16th hole because of damage to the green by proposed work at the quarry face!

It is interesting to note that by April 1911, Mr Knaggs had become a member of the Bamburgh Parish Council and of their committee to arrange celebrations for the Coronation of King George V. Presumably he also kept the members acquainted with developments at the quarry and allayed any fears that they might have had.

The *Alnwick Gazette* of 20th May, 1911 reported the departure of the first shipload of whinstone from the Budle pier which was supposed to have left on 13th but actually left on the 17th. The vessel was the *Gangeren* which was laden with a cargo for Felixstowe. Its departure was held up by the breaking of a 'plate' on a steam crane necessitating a new one being obtained from Glasgow. In the event the ship ran aground in the shallows but was refloated at the next high tide and sailed, undamaged, on its way.

In late June the Belford Rural District Council received from Brand's the details of the cottages to be erected for the men at 'Budle Bay Quarry'. The Surveyor, having examined the plans, said that they were in accordance with

Right: This photograph of the quarry face at Kitling Hill quarry was taken in 2010. During the quarry's period of operation there was a locomotive shed, a workshop, stores and other buildings to house tools and equipment at this site. All trace of these has disappeared.

Author

Below: This commercial picture postcard, dating from the 1950s, shows the site of the 'zig-zag' which allowed locomotives to move between the upper level tracks, linking the quarry with the stone crusher, and the lower level tracks along which the crushed stone was taken to the jetty seen here on the right-hand side.

Author's Collection

local bylaws except for the method of sewage disposal which would be of danger to the mussels in Budle Bay. On the same day there was a report of several of the workmen at the quarry having been struck by lightning, though none was seriously hurt!

By July the quarry was described as 'working briskly' producing broken stone for road making. The reconstruction of the old pier was said to be complete with one or two vessels being loaded every week.

The quarry tramway, or railway, was operated in two parts. The first was for transporting the stone from the quarry to the crushers for a distance of over half a mile across the golf course above the sea cliffs. The second part, located at a lower level, was for moving the crushed stone from the hoppers below the crushers to the quay for loading onto the moored vessels. The two parts of the system were joined by a zig-zag of track on steep gradients between the two levels. All locomotives were normally kept overnight at the shed near to the quarry and one accessed the lower level via the zig-zag each day. The precise location of the shed has not been identified.

The track was laid to 3 ft gauge on wooden sleepers. It was lightly ballasted using crushed stone from the quarry. A newspaper report describes the first locomotive to operate on the upper part of the line as being called *Mary*. This locomotive was recalled by a local 'gaffer', Mr Cowe of Greenhill, when interviewed in the 1950s by an authority on industrial railways, the late Harold Bowtell. Mr Cowe recalled *Mary* as also having worked on the quayside, until the arrival of a second locomotive.

Mary was a Kerr, Stuart 0-4-0 tank locomotive (Works No. KS705), which was built in 1901. It was one of two supplied new, for 2 ft gauge track, to T.A. Martin for use in India, though possibly not going there. It weighed about 6½ tons, had 6 in. x 10 in. cylinders and was originally called *Begum*. It belonged to the 'Sirdar' class of locomotives built by Kerr, Stuart in Staffordshire in an attempt to compete with other manufacturers in the 'quarry market'. It possessed 'short square side tanks' according to information given locally to the late Harold Bowtell in the 1950s. It was returned to Kerr, Stuart's works in 1903 and regauged to 3 ft. It was sold to J.A. McClean of Oban, Scotland, and used at Balvicar Quarry. McClean's became bankrupt and the quarry closed in 1911. After arrival at Budle (by the 17th May, 1911 and possibly from a quarry in Argyll) it carried the name *Mary*, being painted, according to the newspaper report, in bright green and vermilion. *Mary* was initially used on the upper section of the line, though a photograph exists of it shunting wagons on the quayside. Later it shunted the quarry. It apparently returned to Scotland in 1916 or 1917; this fits in with the closure of the quarries at Budle for the duration of the World War. It was certainly not present when Brand's Budle plant and machinery was sold in 1918. Later it is recorded in the ownership of the Lanarkshire County Council during the construction of Camps Reservoir near Crawford (1916-1930), where it continued to bear the name *Mary*. It was included in a sale of plant at Camps in July 1949 and is presumed to have been scrapped some time after this date by J.N. Connell, a scrap merchant at Coatbridge.

During his visit to Bamburgh in the 1950s Harold Bowtell was provided with

This is a digitally modified picture, based on the works photograph of sister locomotive *Sirdar*, suggesting how *Mary* might have appeared if delivered new to Brands by the locomotive builders Kerr, Stuart & Co. *Mary* sported a livery of bright green and vermilion whilst at Bamburgh. *The Hunslet Engine Company (Kerr, Stuart Archive collection), courtesy of Henry Noon*

The small locomotive on the jetty at Budle is *Mary*, the 'Sirdar' class locomotive, which appears to be shunting a pair of tipper wagons. The engine is dwarfed by the two large cranes (built by Smith's of Leeds) and the steamer which has arrived to take on a cargo of crushed stone. Much dredging would be required today to permit such a vessel to approach this jetty!

Jack Birkett Collection

some details of the other locomotives by Mr Cowe, and by a Charlie Hood of the golf club who claimed to have ridden on, and driven, *Mary*.

The second locomotive used at Budle was an unnamed 0-4-0 saddle tank locomotive, built by William Bagnall's (Works No. WB1478/1896). It had 6 in. x 9 in. outside cylinders, a circular firebox and was fitted with Baguley valve gear. It arrived at Budle some time in 1911 from the ownership of the Glasgow Iron & Steel Co., Wishaw, who had owned the locomotive since new. It is said to have worked in the 'Melting Shop' there. It was advertised as 'for sale' from Wishaw in the *The Engineer* of 11th September, 1909 along with two sister engines. It bore the number '16' whilst at Wishaw but appears to have carried no number whilst at Budle. On 9th June, 1913 spares for the locomotive were supplied to Charles Brand but another order, dated 20th April, 1914 was cancelled. This would be as a result of the Budle locomotives being out-of-use when quarrying declined and then ceased near to the outbreak of war. The locomotive was advertised, by Shirlaw Allan & Co. in the *Contract Journal* of 5th June, 1918, as part of the Brand's plant and machinery to be sold, later that month, on 14th June. By 23rd September it had passed into the hands of the dealer, J.F. Wake of Darlington, where, apparently, it had a new chimney fitted. It is likely that it was the Bagnall 3 ft gauge saddle tank advertised as 'for sale' by Wake's in the *Contract Journal* of 13th November, 1918. This locomotive was described as 'small, cabless and like a chip potato carrier' during Harold Bowtell's visit to the area in the 1950s! It was the locomotive that was the first choice for moving the wagons of crushed stone from the hoppers to the quay.

The third locomotive at Budle was, appropriately, named *Budle Crag*. Its works photograph survives in the Glasgow University Archives. It was built at Kilmarnock by Andrew Barclay & Co. (Works No. 1249/1911), and dispatched to Budle on 25th July, 1911. It was thus new (some might say 'brand new'!) when it arrived at Budle via Belford station. It had two outside cylinders measuring 10 in. x 16 in. (or 10 in. x 18 in. in some sources). It worked on the upper part of the system moving wagons between the quarry and the crushers. The last spares delivered to Brand's for this locomotive were in July 1914. Later in 1917 it left Budle, being transferred to the Board of Trade, Timber Supplies Department, for use by the 120th Company of the Canadian Forestry Corps working at Altyre Woods, south of Forres, Elgin. Even later (by June 1918) it was with the 122nd Company at Forres. Spares for this locomotive were sent to Nairn in Scotland in June 1920. A surviving photograph shows it, still carrying the name *Budle Crag*, at work at Forres. Later it is known to have worked at Camps Reservoir, then for Richard Baillie, contractor, on various jobs in the Lammermuir Hills. Then, in about 1935, it was moved to the Peak District of Derbyshire where it was still in existence in 1946-47. Its name was still faintly visible on the side tanks in the 1930s. During the reservoir construction contract at Ladybower, in the Peak District, it gained a reputation for coming off the track easily, and being very difficult to rerail! It is believed to have been broken up at the end of the Derbyshire part of its career.

Little is known of the type and number of the wagons used at Budle apart from that they were metal-bodied tipper wagons of two ton capacity. At least one siding was provided close to the quarry for the empty wagons awaiting

This is the official works photograph of *Budle Crag* (Works No. AB 1249/1911) built by Andrew Barclay at the Caledonia Works in Kilmarnock, Scotland. Brands' bought the locomotive new from this company. It was delivered by rail to Belford station and thence by road to Bamburgh.
Andrew Barclay Archive, University of Glasgow

The former trackbed now forms a public footpath across the course of the Bamburgh Golf Club. The dark colour of the path arises from the cinders and gravel that were used to ballast the track. The stone crusher at the end of the path was demolished and replaced by a wartime gun emplacement overlooking Budle Bay.   *Author*

loading. Several sidings served the various parts of the quarry face. After they were loaded the locomotive would have marshalled its train of wagons ready for the start of the journey to the crushers which involved an initial upwards climb to reach the summit of the line through some very shallow cuttings. Then it would have been necessary to apply the locomotive brakes as the train of wagons pushed it down the gradient towards the crushers. Here the cutting sides were up to 20 ft deep on the landward side and 10 ft on the seaward side. Wind-blown sand often covered the ballast on this section of the line, just as it often covers the present-day footpath. Eventually the train of wagons would cross over the points leading to the zig-zag and arrive at the embankment loop and siding where the crushers were ready to receive the stone. No elevators were needed and gravity was sufficient for the stone to be tipped from the wagons, crushed and screened before being loaded into wagons on the lower section of the system. Here a second engine would haul or propel the wagons onto the quay ready for the crane to lift them and tip their contents into the hold of the waiting vessel.

The quarrying at Budle Crag appears to have been regarded as somewhat of a 'model' enterprise for on 23rd September, 1911 Mr Knaggs met a party of about 30 surveyors who had travelled all of the way from London to view the site! They were met at Belford station, taken by road to the quarry and then they inspected the whole system. Afterwards they were provided with a lunch at the Bamburgh Castle Hotel before being returned to Belford to catch their London train.

The names of vessels departing from the quay with loads of stone are well documented in the local newspapers. It appears that there were several involved in this traffic. Amongst the first vessels to call regularly were the SS *Wharfedale*, *Slateford*, *Glenconnor* and *Glenrose*. Newspaper records indicate that calls were made by other larger vessels including the SS *Inchbrayock*, *Dunleith*, *Ferrum*, *Dot* and *Silford*. Others, including the SS *Zephyr*, *Glenbrook*, *Gleno* and *Argentum* made occasional visits. From time to time vessels collected smaller loads of stone; lighters such as the *Rhoda* and the *Nero* took stone to Newcastle, for example, and *Leda* took stone to Middlesbrough.

A large majority of the stone shipments was to ports in the east and south-east of England. Boston (Lincolnshire), Rochester, Whitstable, Great Yarmouth, Kings Lynn, Grimsby, Felixstowe and Southwold received many shipments. In the case of the deliveries to the Kentish ports, they resulted from a decision made by the Kent County Council in the early 1900s that all of the main roads in the county were to be surfaced with tarmacadam. Accordingly cargoes of stone were received at Rochester and Whitstable harbours and then loaded onto rail wagons for distribution to wherever the stone was needed. Much of that arriving at Whitstable; for example, was moved over the former Canterbury & Whitstable railway line for use in the Canterbury district.

Sometimes a single vessel would visit Budle Quay as many as four or five times in the month, for example the *Ferrum* took away five cargoes of stone for Grimsby in April 1913. The same month *Slateford* took four loads for Boston and *Dot* four loads for Kings Lynn. Up to 15 loads could be exported in any one calendar month, however the demand for stone in the winter months was somewhat less than in the summer.

Whilst most of the stone from Budle Crag is known to have left by vessel, smaller quantities are known to have left the quarry by road. One of the contracting concerns known to have been involved was the firm of J. & J. Murdy of Chathill which owned a traction engine named *Northumbrian Chief*. This hauled loads of stone from Budle to the sidings at Belford station for onward movement by the North Eastern Railway.

To facilitate the exit of loaded vessels from the bay, Brand's proposed some improvements to the water channels. In early 1912 they submitted plans for the building of a groin, or retaining wall, to be built alongside the low water channel of the Budle Water at Budle Point and jutting into the Bay. The aim was for the water to be channelled so as to concentrate the flow, have a scouring action and thus maintain a good depth; the walls would prevent sand and mud from sliding down. These walls were to be made of two lines of woven brushwood with a pebble and stone filling. The stone was to be quarried from the headland at Budle Point. Letters from the Board of Trade to the Belford District Council in February 1912 invited comments on the matter. The plans seemed in order as far as the council was concerned and no objections were raised. Permission to proceed was given provided that the work was completed by 1st May, 1915. In the event it would seem that this scheme was not a great success for just 18 months later, in December 1913, the *Berwick Advertiser* contained an article reporting that Brand's had new plans. They proposed to build an overhead line or cableway direct from the quarries to Holy Island to 'give greater facilities for the shipment of stone'. Despite their efforts, Brand's had not been able to improve the channels and vessels were still only able to enter and leave Budle Creek at high tide. Brand's felt that Holy Island harbour would firstly be more sheltered and secondly vessels would be able to enter and leave at 'all states of the tide'. The 'transporter', as it was referred to, would have been between four and four and a half miles in length and would have eliminated the need for a railway system outside the quarry.

However, these plans came to naught because the onset of World War I in 1914 brought the quarrying and shipment of stone to a halt. Many of the men left to join the army or to work elsewhere. Some stone remained in store at Budle, as in February 1918 Brand's were contacted by the council's surveyor, Mr Dodd, regarding the price they would want for 2,500 tons of road materials and 1,000 tons of 'clippings'. Brand's preferred that the council make an offer. The surveyor reported to the council that using their own carts the carting of this quantity would be 'out of the question' but that he hoped to arrange an offer of engine haulage. In the event the removal of the stone, by road lorry, was started in March 1918. After a brief pause in May, the removal of the stone was completed.

Just one fatality was reported at the quarry. On the 30th August, 1913 two workers, William Pollard and William Weatherstone were working together filling rail wagons at the foot of the face. At 10 o'clock in the morning there was a fall of stone. Pollard, who had only recently arrived from Ipswich to work at the quarry, was crushed and fatally injured by a large piece of stone which had fallen some 20 ft. Weatherstone was slightly more fortunate. Despite receiving a fractured skull and the crushing of the toes of his right foot, he survived. There were others who also received serious injuries. A verdict of 'accidental death' was recorded with the accident caused by an unusually heavy fall of rain loosening the rock, despite the face having appeared normal when inspected before the day's work started.

Quarrying did not resume after the end of the war, Brand's plant and machinery from Budle having been sold in June 1918. However a brick construction to the left of the fifth fairway still survives; this was one of the two powder houses associated with the quarry. A lean-to was erected against it in 1922 as a shelter for golfers.

Today a public footpath exists along the line of the railway's trackbed and much of the gravel ballast is still present. Permission needs to be sought from the golf club to make a deviation to inspect the quarry face. At the site of the crushers there has been much change as, at the start of World War II, a huge concrete and brick gun emplacement was constructed on the embankment, with a view to the defence of the Bay in the event of enemy invasion. This edifice still survives above the remains of the screen foundations. The junction of the zig-zag line can be identified though shifting sand makes the task of identifying the rest of the lower part of the system rather difficult. The quay, now once again in considerable disrepair, survives though no trace of the rails can be seen. In the 1950s the railway's line of approach to the quay formed part of a small caravan site. A short distance from the site of the crushers and screens exists a small building reputed to have been an office of Brand's. This area is now prone to flooding after heavy rain. It can also be approached via the public right of way leading down from the Bamburgh to Waren Mill road.

The Howick Estate records show that Mr Knaggs, whilst supervising the quarries at Budle, had paid a visit to Craster to investigate the possibility of opening up a new quarry for Brand's there. Apparently this proposal involved the extraction of 40,000 tons per year! George Grey, the Land Agent for the Howick Estate, where the quarry would have been created, informed Knaggs that there was no chance at all of shipping that quantity of stone from Craster. Not surprisingly, the scheme was not proceeded with.

This 2011 photograph, taken almost 100 years after operations ceased here, shows the surviving bases of Brand's crushing and screening plant at the end of the railway line from Kitling Hill. One of the small locomotives moved crushed stone from this point to the jetty to be craned into coastal steamers. Some left the site by road lorry.   *Author*

Alnwick's newspaper, the *Northumberland Gazette*, illustrated an article on Brunton's wagonway with two pen and ink sketches, both reproduced here. The first shows the line from Spindlestone still under construction, where it approaches the road at the side of Budle Bay. The line was single-tracked though the drawing seems to show some evidence of points for a siding or loop at this point.   *The Northumberland Gazette*

The second of the two sketches shows the view in the opposite direction with the rails following the foreshore towards Brunton's new jetty which projected into Budle Bay. Note the wooden-bodied tipper wagons on the right. The edifice on the skyline in the centre is not Bamburgh Castle, as has been suggested, but is probably the crushing works of Brand's separate quarry system.   *The Northumberland Gazette*

7 - *Brunton's Waren (Budle Bay) Waggonway*

The second of the railways in the Bamburgh area with Scottish connections was constructed by the quarrying concern of Messrs Brunton & Sons, based in North Queensferry, Fife, Scotland.

Alexander Brunton, the son of the quarry owner and contractor who had built the Wallace Monument, was born in Strathkinness, Fife, in 1856. By 1881 he had become an engine fitter and lived in Edinburgh. Within a few years he had assumed control, with his brother Adam, of the quarrying business from his father and was described, in various places, as a quarry owner or quarrymaster. From the end of the 19th century they traded as 'Messrs Brunton and Sons' and operated out of Carlingnose Quarry adjacent to the Firth of Forth.

A sale of the Spindlestone Estate at Budle, near Bamburgh, took place on 26th July, 1910. It was reported in the local newspaper, the *Berwick Advertiser*, four days later. Brunton spent £12,000 on the purchase of part of this Estate for quarrying purposes. The newspaper reported: 'It is the intention of the purchaser to open up the quarries on the property on a large scale. It is expected that employment will be found for about six hundred men. It is stated that a solid seam of rock of some two miles has been discovered'.

The same newspaper, dated 20th January, 1911 reported that the surveyor of the Belford Rural District Council had received a letter from 'Messrs Alex Brunton and Son' asking for permission to lay a line of rails across the highway at 'Budle Bay, near Waren Mill'. The letter stated that it was the intention that the rails should be laid from the proposed new whinstone quarry on the east side of the highway at Budle. The line was to emerge onto the highway having crossed the fields known as 'West Sea Lands' and 'Lisle's Field'. A loading pier was to be constructed in Budle Bay. The company proposed to take precautions about public safety at the crossing! The surveyor agreed to meet with Brunton's representative at the site so that more definite plans could be laid before the Council at their next meeting. The same details were reported in the Alnwick newspaper of 21st January.

The *Alnwick and County Gazette* of 11th February, 1911, under the headline of 'Bamburgh, The New Industries', reported that it was the intention of 'the recent purchaser of the estate' to work the rock that faced the road and that the stone would be transported along a line of rails flanking the beach at Budle Bay to a new pier near to the oyster beds.

> It is many a long day since so many navigators [referring to the labourers or 'navvies'] and other men were at work in this district, and the old corn mill will again witness ships coming up this summer along the dredged channel of the Waren stream. Huts and cottages will soon have to be found for the two hundred men engaged in the developments.

The Ordnance Survey maps of the 1920s identify the small quarry on the flank of Spindlestone Hill (NU 148343) plus the route of the waggonway, the site of the road crossing, and the section of the line along part of the shore known as 'The Bight' leading towards Kiln Point (NU 153352).

The *Berwick Advertiser* newspaper of 3rd February (and the *Alnwick and County Gazette* of 4th February) contained details of the surveyor's report to the council under the headline 'The New Quarries'. He reported that he had met with Brunton's representative who had told him that they wished to construct a level crossing with rails crossing the highway at an oblique angle. It was intended that a lookout man would always be on duty to check that the highway was clear of traffic and to warn any person before any wagons were allowed to cross the highway. The wagons would be horse-drawn across the highway for several months until the railway was made strong enough to carry the weight of a locomotive. The surveyor, Mr Lake, thought that it was important that a 'Caution' sign be erected at the site. It was Brunton's representative's opinion that a locomotive at the side of the highway would not be any more dangerous to horse traffic than the motor traffic on it. He considered that the erection of a stone wall or fence to separate the road from the trackbed (where, for a short distance, they ran parallel) was not necessary. The question of the crossing of three public rights of way was also discussed by Brunton's representative and the surveyor. Brunton's would do what was required to keep these routes open to the public.

The Chairman of the council's committee considered that the matter should be carefully dealt with and that a paper agreement should be drawn up: 'it is our duty to look after the interests of the public'. The clerk to the committee and the surveyor were instructed to look after the necessary arrangements.

The council's committee also discussed the question of the width of a roadway where the Budle lifeboat could require access to the bay, the width proposed by Brunton being considered too narrow. Midst laughter it was stated that the lifeboat had not actually been launched since 1874! Three other level crossings located along the proposed line were also discussed. (It was obviously considered necessary for several roadways to exist to facilitate possible launchings of the lifeboat as Brand's had been asked to solve the same problem.)

By the 17th May, 1911 the local newspapers had reported once again on Brunton's activities. At that time they were constructing the tramway using tip-wagons and horses. The trackbed was being excavated towards the rock cliffs where the quarry was to be located. Clay and other debris were being tipped along the shoreline and this was to continue along the foreshore for 1½ miles into Budle Bay. There was sufficient depth of water for the construction of a new pier at the mouth of the Waren Water. A certain Alex Bell, with some 15 years' experience of working for Brunton, was the 'pioneer' of the enterprise. A body of men, currently working at a quarry in Fife, Scotland, was to be transferred to Waren where they would produce setts and crushed roadstone for transport by sea to English ports (using steam boats of 500 tons). This would involve the use of half a dozen stone crushers and the employment of 150 men. The proprietors planned to build a dozen cottages to house these men, with others to follow. The wage bill was said to be between £400 and £500 per fortnight at that time.

The *Berwick Advertiser* of 1st September, 1911 reported that a sub-committee of the council had met with Mr Brunton himself regarding the plans for the embankment and tramway alongside Budle Bay. Brunton stated that his company would meet all of the Council's requirements regarding the rights of way which were to be shown on the agreement which was being drawn up. The council Minutes recorded that the plans should be sent to the Board of Trade.

A copy of the agreement, dated 13th September, 1911 between the Belford Rural District Council and Messrs Brunton & Son, survives in the Berwick Record Office. Brunton's are described as the owners of 'Waren Mill Quarry'. It was drawn up by Adam Douglas, solicitors, of Alnwick. The agreement included reference to 'the purpose of sending along such rails, wagons containing stone from the said quarry, such wagons to be propelled first by horses and subsequently by mechanical power'. The accompanying map shows the area of the proposed quarry as lying due east of Waren House, on the side of East Hill between the 100 ft and 200 ft contours. The agreement permitted Brunton's to lay the rails at right angles across the highway (and similarly at other public rights of way), to make good the land at the side of the rails and to erect and maintain two gates (to close off the tramway when no wagons were passing). It was agreed that they should maintain the road for 3 ft on each side of the crossing and that danger signals and lights should be displayed. Furthermore Brunton's agreed to erect a wall or fence at the side of the track if any injury should arise from an accident. They agreed to erect two notice boards and not to operate wagons over the crossing between one hour after sunset and one hour before sunrise unless a red light was carried on the rear of the wagons. They agreed to indemnify the council against any claims. The council would be allowed to close the line and take up the rails if there was any reported nuisance! Both sides agreed to give one months notice of any intention to terminate the agreement. Finally Brunton's agreed to pay a rental of £2 per year to the council and to pay all expenses associated with the drawing up of the agreement.

The Board of Trade received copies of the plans associated with the tramway and the proposed new jetty. The plans and accompanying documentation provide much precise information about the nature of the track to be laid, the embankment and the proposed jetty. The architects for the scheme were Messrs Dickson, Archer & Thorpe of Alnwick.

The rails used were to be of 5½ in. in depth and were to be laid on wooden sleepers of depth 4 in. and width 7½ in. The sleepers were to be laid at a spacing of 3 ft 4 in. and the gauge of the track was to be 3 ft. Guard timbers were to be provided at the road crossing and they were to measure 5 in. by 4 in.

The embankment was to have water-drainage culverts at Waren Mill and Kiln Point and was to be 3 ft 3 in. above the high water mark for spring tides. The central portion of the embankment, carrying the waggonway [sic] was to be 12 ft in width. The sides of the embankment were to consist of hand-set rough pitching laid at an angle of 45 degrees. Access to the beach at one of the public crossings (near Kiln Point) was to be on a gradient of 1 in 16, with the land made level to the public road on the other side.

The proposals included the new 'wharf' to be constructed near the mouth of Budle Water. The jetty proposed was to be 300 ft in length with a width of 31 ft. It was to carry two roads for the stone wagons with a crane road (of standard gauge. The craneway and one of the stone wagon roads would be laid as mixed gauge track. The whole was to be substantially built with 12 in. square vertical

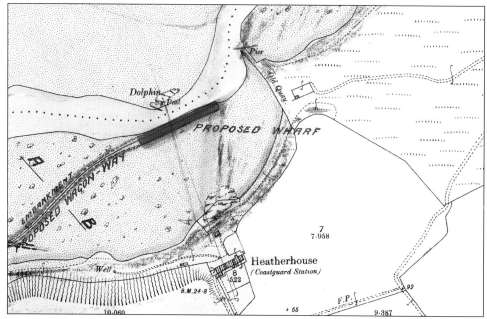

The Northumberland County Record Office holds the extensive written details and plans for Brunton's quarrying system, including this view which shows the 'Proposed Wharf'. These plans were drawn up before the competitors, Brand's, had laid their railways to the 'Pier' and 'Old Quay' shown towards the right hand side of the picture.

Northumberland County Record Office

This photograph, taken in the snowy winter of 2010/11, shows the route of Brunton's wagonway from the Spindlestone cliffs (*on the right of the picture*) towards the edge of Budle Bay. The line of rails followed the line of small trees shown descending the hillside (just above the picture's mid-line) towards the Belford to Bamburgh road. *Author*

timbers with 12 in. x 6 in. timbers for the fenders. Horizontal timbers were to measure 12 in. x 6 in. at 10 ft intervals. Diagonal braces measuring 9 in. by 4 in. would reinforce the structure. The upper surface was to be covered with 4 in. x 1 in. planking. The embankment, itself, was to be extended into the bay, to join the wharf, opposite the coastguard station.

The Board of Trade gave their consent to the construction upon conditions that the work be completed within five years. After the date of 21st January, 1918 the consent would be considered to be null and void.

At this point it is pertinent to raise the question as to how much of these proposed works were carried out. Some quarrying certainly took place at the quarry at Spindlestone. This can be ascertained by comparing the layout shown on the Ordnance Survey maps which immediately pre-dated and post-dated the time of Brunton's occupation. The route of the tramway from the quarry, crossing the road and proceeding along part of the foreshore is marked on the 1920s maps. In addition pen and ink sketches, showing the line in construction were published in a local newspaper. A present-day site inspection reveals the cutting leading from the quarry to the main road and the deposition of much crushed stone along the tramway alignment on an otherwise very muddy shore. This line of stone juts out into the bay towards where the wharf was planned to be built. However, only a few timbers are exposed above the mud today and it is possible that this last part of the project was incomplete. In the records of shipping printed in the local newspapers, no records of any vessels using a 'new wharf' are reported, though the visits of ships to the old grain jetty (used by Messrs Brand) are recorded regularly. It is possible, therefore, that if, as seems possible, the wharf was not completed, then the only stone taken along the line of rails was for the building of the trackbed itself. Any other quarried stone would have been removed by road; this would have included stone purchased by the district council for the local roads. It is certain that the planned permanent housing accommodation for the quarrymen was not proceeded with.

It is frustrating that the local newspapers, some of whose editions have not survived, even in the national archives, make no further reference to the quarry until 1913. Perhaps there was little activity and few developments to report. However, the *Berwick Advertiser* of 28th February, 1913 contained an article under the headline 'Quarry Complication'. The surveyor to the Belford RDC (by now a Mr T.W. Dodd) reported that he had received notice that the gates to Brunton's Quarry had been locked following the instruction of the agent, Mr Clayhills. This act prevented the council from removing stone. Clayhills consented to reopen the gates on the condition that he was paid for the stone taken out. The council had arranged with Messrs Brunton (described as 'the supposed owners') to take out the stone but Clayhills said that the contract with them was not completed. Clayhills' solicitors asked to be informed of the full amount of the stone supplied and the money paid to Mr Branton [sic] and requested a cheque for the stone taken out between March 1912 and March 1913. Nothing had apparently been paid during that time for 'winning royalties' according to the council's surveyor. A confusing situation.

On 28th March, 1913 the same newspapers, under the heading 'The Quarry Dispute', described that the council's surveyor had received a further letter from Mr Clayhills to the effect that, until the money owed was paid, he declined to enter into any contract with the council for supplying stone. The surveyor reported that this would affect the supply of some 900 cubic yards of metal for three groups of roads. A member of the committee, Mr Adamson, said that Messrs Brunton were finished with the quarry, whilst another, Mr Gray, suggested getting the stone from the nearby Brada Quarry. A resolution was passed to this effect.

On 4th July the Berwick newspaper reported that 'The Spindlestone Affair is settled'. The council had paid Mr Clayhills the sum of £11 12s. 10d. and Brunton's the sum of £7 13s. 2d. thus bringing the complex dispute involving the council, Clayhills and Messrs Brunton to an end. This was the last reference made by the newspapers to Brunton's concern and it must be assumed, in view of the Councillor's comment above, that the quarrying activities had ceased in March 1913. The Ordnance Survey maps of the early 1920s indicate that most, if not all, of the tramway had been removed by the time of survey. Alexander Brunton died in the early 1920s.

Today the former small quarry lies on private land but the cutting which the trackbed followed can be seen from the roadside. A gate in the roadside wall indicates the position of the former level crossing. The route of the line can be followed along the edge of the bay and remains of the ballast used on the trackbed form a dark line along the foreshore. Of Brunton's wooden jetty there are few signs, though a few timbers projecting from the mud at the side of the low water channel are probably its remains. Further along the shore, the old jetty, rebuilt by Brand's but now in a poor state of repair, juts out into the bay, though much dredging would be needed for vessels of any substantial size to approach it today!

8 - The Red Barns Quarry Tramway

Red Barns is located to the west of the Seahouses to Bamburgh road (now the B1340) about half a mile south of the entrance to Bamburgh Castle (NU189343). The minor road leading to the quarry leaves the main road near to the southernmost extent of the 'Armstrong Cottages'. Shown as a small quarry on the First Edition Ordnance Survey maps of the 1860s, it had become enlarged by the turn of the century. No quarry records appear to have survived. By the date of publication of the next Ordnance Survey maps in the 1920s the Bamburgh Gasworks had been created towards one side of the quarry. This supplied the village with gas made from coal until the supply of piped natural gas arrived. It is unfortunate that, apart from books of meter-readings and accounts no records of the gas company appear to have been deposited in record offices or retained elsewhere.

Several 'senior' Bamburgh residents have reported that a small tramway once existed within the quarry. Initially it was believed to have been used for moving stone from the quarry faces. Later it was said to have been used for moving coal, delivered to the site by road, to the retort house. Unfortunately no photographs or plans of the rail layout within the quarry have been discovered.

This photograph, taken from the Seahouses to Bamburgh road, shows the present-day residential buildings occupying the former quarry at Red Barns. One of the buildings appears to be derived from the former Retort House, constructed when the quarry was converted to house the local gas works. *Author*

In the early 1890s Lord Armstrong was strongly in favour of a branch being constructed from the North Sunderland Railway (linking Chathill with the village and harbour of Seahouses) to Bamburgh. If the branch had been constructed it has been suggested that the quarry tramway could have been extended to provide a link to branch and thus facilitate the bringing of coal to the gas works. The proposed branch would have left the main North Sunderland line between the school and North Sunderland station (the only intermediate one on the branch) before heading northwards towards Bamburgh. However, this never got beyond the 'proposal' stage.

9 - *The Railway at Brada Quarry*

Today, in the early years of the 21st century, the huge quarry faces at Brada Quarry (NU 162341), close to Bamburgh, are nesting places for gulls mistaking the ledges on the otherwise near vertical surfaces for those on sea cliffs! Quarrying here ceased 50 years ago and today the quarries are visited by only a few: ornithologists watching the bird life, persons seeking to purloin a few stones for a rockery garden or to dump rubbish, or youths trying out their motorcycles on the quarry floor! The quarry forms part of the lands of the local Baker-Cresswell family.

In the first half of the 19th century, whilst it lay on the Howick Estate, Brada Quarry was known as 'Budle New Town Quarry'. A standard gauge railway was proposed in 1828 to link the quarry with the jetty at the side of Budle Bay. However, the railway scheme was not implemented despite a small amount of quarrying taking place (*see Chapter Nine*).

In 1853 a certain Robert Gillies obtained a lease of the quarry, by then known as Budle Whinstone Quarry, from Earl Grey for a period of 20 years. He was to transport his stone to the harbour by cart, no tramway or railway being used. It is not known how long Gillies operated out of the quarry at Budle.

ROLMAC that operated out of Brada Quarry owned several Thorneycroft lorries for leading their stone. This delightful picture shows one of these lorries and is part of the photographic archive of Thornycroft vehicles.   *The Thornycroft Register, via Alan Sleight*

Just one 'vintage' photograph has been traced of the quarry system at Brada Quarry. It is reproduced here and shows the quarry workmen at the quarry in the 1930s. It includes relatives of Fred Wake who supplied the picture. There is a glimpse of a loaded quarry 'tub' between the two men on the right-hand side and of some rail in the foreground.

Fred Wake Collection

Quarrying resumed here on a small scale at the start of the 20th century. In March 1912, for example, the *Berwick Advertiser* reported a quarryman breaking his thigh in an accident. Then, in 1913, a Belford councillor suggested using Brada Quarry as a source of road metalling. Some four years later it was reported that four or five men were engaged in working the whinstone. At this time the Brada Quarry was part of the estate owned by the Cruddas family but the Lessee has not been identified.

The first documentary evidence of the start of substantial quarrying appears in the form of a lease drawn up for the ROLMAC Supply Co. in 1933. ROLMAC was a company formed by Roland McLaren and Hilda Mary McLaren, who operated quarries at Belford and elsewhere. ('ROLMAC' was a combination of the first syllable of each of Roland's names.) Its registered address was 'Singleton House, Northumberland'. John Clark of Haltwhistle was a partner in the company. ROLMAC was subsequently acquired by the Amalgamated Roadstone Corporation (ARC) in 1940, this, in turn, becoming part of the Hanson Group of companies in 1989.

In April 1935 ROLMAC installed new crushing and screening plant. A 2 ft gauge railway line of just less than 200 yards in length was laid between the quarry face and a rope-worked incline leading to the crushers and screens. Some of the rails were portable and removed between the various quarry faces. The stone was extracted in the 'usual' way: a hydraulic drill was used to drill holes into the stone, with black powder being used as an explosive to bring down part of the quarry face. Loading of the stone wagons was performed manually by the quarrymen using shovels. The crushers were electrically powered, the supply being supplied by the Newcastle & District Electricity Co. in the first instance. The crushed stone was taken away from the quarry by lorries and used mainly for making tarmacadam, but also as a road dressing. ROLMAC owned a number of 4- and 6-wheeled Thornycroft lorries which delivered stone locally. Other stone was taken away by a haulier named Smiles whose vehicles bore the legend 'Smiles for Miles'. At this time ROLMAC employed 25 men who were active in the quarrying process. In addition there were electricians, joiners and an office manager and foreman.

For just over eight years small locomotives were used to shunt the short trains of side-tipper wagons. There were two locomotives at Brada. Both were small 4-wheeled petrol-engined machines with mechanical transmission obtained new from R. & A. Lister of Dursley, Gloucestershire. The first to be used had the Works Number L6572 and was built in 1935. The second was L7645 built in 1936. The former carried the running number LM11, whilst the latter was numbered LM12. The locomotives performed considerable work as records show that crushed stone production at Brada rose from just over 23,000 tons per annum in the mid-1930s to over 52,000 tons in 1941! However, in 1944, for some unknown reason, perhaps because of a marked decline in orders during wartime or shortage of spare parts, the locomotives ceased working and they were put into store. The small tubs of stone were moved by hand after this time. The tubs employed in the quarry were metal-bodied four-wheeled side tippers each holding about 2 cwt of stone.

LM11 subsequently worked in a granite quarry near Builth Wells in Radnorshire in the 1950s, finally being scrapped in 1961, but the fate of the other

A careful search reveals the site of various quarry 'remains' including the crusher and lorry loading facility. In several places, in the undergrowth at the sides of the quarry are several lengths of the lightweight rail used on ROLMAC's narrow gauge system at Brada, which have escaped the attention of the scrapman! *(Both) Author*

Brada Quarry forms part of the estate of the Baker-Cresswell family but is used, unofficially, by walkers, bird watchers, youngsters learning how to motorcycle, and others. The quarry faces form the nest sites for numerous seabirds mistaking them for seaside cliffs. *Author*

locomotive is not known; it disappeared from Brada in about 1953 after a long period of disuse. Stone extraction from the quarry finally ceased in about 1955. The remaining plant, the wagons and the rails were eventually sold. Remarkably, perhaps because of the infrequency of map updates, the quarry's railway, though clearly already disused for some years, did not appear on the large scale Ordnance Survey maps until the 1960s! Furthermore it is still featured on the 1980s series of maps though the track had been long-removed by this time!

The lease on the quarry was varied in 1961 to allow limestone to be imported to, and stored at, the site. The final lease was issued in May 1972, expiring 10 years later.

The quarry now lies on the private land of the Baker-Cresswell Estate and access for vehicles is discouraged by the placing of some large boulders at its entrance. Remains of a weigh house and loading banks survive as do the concrete bases of some of the quarry equipment.

10 - The Crag Mill Quarry Railway, Belford

Belford is a village located approximately mid-way between Alnwick and Berwick. Originally the Great North Road passed through the village centre but the present-day A1 road forms a by-pass on its eastern side. A few hundred yards further to the east lies the main Newcastle to Edinburgh railway: the East Coast main line.

Two large quarries are located close to Belford. On its eastern side lies Eastington Quarry, which has had, for many years, a connection with the main line. Though permission was given to Messrs Appleby Ltd, in a lease of 1915 to use 'tramways, roads and railways', it appears that this option was not taken up, though the *Alnwick Gazette* of 6th October, 1928 referred to the concern as 'laying a light railway from Belford to the coast' and employing 100 men for the purpose. Remains of the line cannot be found and no maps or documents record its existence. The standard gauge line, linking sidings at Belford with the quarry, has always been worked as a siding by locomotives of the main railway companies rather than industrial ones. As such it is not part of our story.

To the north of the village lies Crag Mill Quarry, named after Cragmill Hill to the east. This whinstone quarry was started to the north of what is now Cragmill Road, linking the old Great North Road (now North Bank) with the modern A1 (NU 111345). At the junction of North Bank and Cragmill Road can be found 'Neralcm', the present-day home of William McLaren, the son of the former quarry operator. (Try reading the house name backwards!)

The Crag Mill Quarry was started around the mid-1920s. A Minute in the county council's Roads & Bridges Committee records that on 25th October, 1926 McLaren's supplied tarred whinstone at 14s. per ton at Crag Mill Quarry for the Berwick and Cornhill Road. (Earlier consignments of stone for the same project and for the Norham to Shoreswood Road were supplied from unspecified quarries, which may or may not have included Crag Mill.) In the following years (apart from a short time in 1930 when they were temporarily deleted from the list of suppliers) Messrs McLaren continued to provide stone for the county council highway projects including the Alnwick to Eglingham Road. In

No photographs or documents have surfaced depicting or describing the quarry rail system at Crag Mill, Belford, with its interesting locomotives. However, this poor quality image shows one of McLaren's Bedford stone-delivery lorries against a background of part of the quarry plant.

Author's Collection

The Whitcomb locomotives appear to have avoided the lenses of photographers whilst they were working at Crag Mill. However, one extremely poor quality photograph has been discovered of locomotive 12028 of 1925 whilst it was working in Northumberland. This was taken at Cawfields Quarry near Hexham, some time before it was moved to Belford. It was previously used to illustrate an article in the *Industrial Railway Record* and was originally copied from a print in an unknown magazine by author Les Charlton.   *Industrial Railway Society*

addition stone from Crag Mill was taken by road to Willington Quay, Newcastle, from whence it was shipped for use in London. There was formerly a siding, known as Crag Mill siding, located close to the station and level crossing on the adjacent main line and some stone was taken from Belford by this route. In 1913, prior to the opening of Crag Mill Quarry, the records of the NER indicate that some 2,239 tons of stone were shipped by rail from Belford though it is not known for certain which local quarry furnished this stone, though it was probably the rail-linked Eastington Quarry.

Crag Mill quarry was formerly operated much in the same way as other local whinstone quarries. The stone was blasted from the quarry face using black powder. The lumps of stone were lifted into small tipper wagons which were propelled by locomotives to the elevators for lifting into the crushers. After crushing the stone was screened into material of various sizes. McLaren's laid a 2 ft gauge internal rail system within the quarry to link the faces and elevators. Unfortunately no maps or plans appear to exist showing the extent of the railway but the tracks are reported to have been moved and extended as the quarry developed. Three locomotives are known to have worked on the system though it has not been discovered if a special shed was constructed to house them.

The locomotives were all 40 horsepower 4-wheeled petrol-mechanical machines built by the Whitcomb Locomotive Co. of Rochelle, Illinois, USA. They had been delivered new to Sir W.G. Armstrong for use in Jamaica, but were returned to the UK after the collapse of a sugar cane scheme made them redundant. Two apparently came to Crag Mill direct from Armstrong's but the third arrived via the Alston Whinstone Co. at Cawfields Quarry, whose railway was nominally 1 ft 11½ in. gauge and was located on Hadrian's Wall at Haltwhistle, to the west of Hexham. (Quarrying at this site completely destroyed a section of the famous Roman wall!) This last locomotive had apparently been rebuilt with a diesel engine. Their works numbers are believed to have been Wcb11827/1924, 11828/1924 and 12028/1925. In the absence of surviving quarry records dating from the period the precise dates of operation of the locomotives have not been discovered. However there is one clue as to the date of arrival of the third Whitcomb. Cawfields Quarry had been operated by the Newcastle Granite & Whinstone Co. until it went into liquidation in 1930, when the Alston Whinstone Co. took over. The third locomotive came from this latter firm and must, therefore, have been bought by McLaren's after 1930. It was certainly recorded at Crag Mill in 1936. McLaren family memories can throw no additional light onto any of the dates and no quarrymen from the 'railway' period survive. The subsequent fate of the locomotives is not apparently known; they were presumably either sold for further use or scrapped.

Stone from the quarry was always removed by road and McLaren's maintained a small fleet of lorries for the purpose. The quarry, much enlarged, is still in operation in the 21st century for Cemex Aggregates North East. (McLaren's ceased to be the operators at the end of the 1980s.) Roadside notices still warn of the dangerous nature of the site and the possibility of noise from blasting operations. Today, however, conveyors and elevators supply the crushing plant and screens, rather than a railway. Huge articulated vehicles transport away the crushed stone along the adjacent A1 road.

Right: Brownieside Quarry appears on the skyline to the centre and right of this picture which was taken from the far side of the nearby A1 road. The railway, linking the quarry and a loading bank at the side of the former A1, now the service road to the houses, followed the line of the coniferous trees to the left.

Author

Below: Brownieside is another of Northumberland's quarries to see only intermittent use. This picture was taken of the inside of the quarry in 2010 and shows part of one of the quarry faces. Unfortunately the main face is almost always in shadow making photography very difficult.

Author

11 - The Brownieside Quarry Railway

Brownieside (formerly Brownyside) Quarry lies at the edge of Tynely (formerly Tinely) Moor just within the boundary of the Berwick District (NU 163236). The milepost which marks the midpoint between Belford and Alnwick lies nearby at the side of the Great North Road, now the A1. From the quarry it is seven miles, by road, to each of the two places named. The altitude of a triangulation point located just above and to the north west of the quarry is shown as 151 metres on modern maps. The quarry is located on the private land of the Frater family of Tynely Farm who have farmed there for several generations, the farm formerly being part of the Ellingham Estate until its sale in the 1980s. Unfortunately the estate records do not contain items relating to the early years of the quarry. The quarry has a reputation for the supply of fine quality sandstone.

The quarry is shown on the earliest Ordnance Survey maps and was linked to the Great North Road by an unfenced track leading down the hillside, reaching the roadside just to the north of the Masons' Arms public house. By the end of the 19th century, and even at the end of the first quarter of the 20th century, maps show that the quarry was hardly any larger! A plan, dated July 1914 and held in the Northumberland Record Office, relates to a survey conducted by George Broadway, architect and surveyor. Whilst showing the quarry in detail it does not indicate a railway. However, this specially drawn plan may have been created prior to resumption of quarrying. Later maps, published up until the 1970s, are based on the 1890s survey and no changes are shown near to the quarry. However, later surveys resulted in the quarry being marked 'Disused' on the 1980s-published maps. The same map records the existence of a 'Police Office' by the side of the A1 road. Observations dating from the 1930s, later recalled by a Belford resident in a taped interview, referred to the quarry railway terminating behind this building.

Today there is another gated track, running approximately south east-north west which climbs the hillside from the old A1 alignment (to the south of the former public house) leading to the entrance to the quarry. Inspection of the quarry in 2009, using this access, showed that there had been some 'recent' quarrying. The sign on the gate protecting the track to the quarry displays a notice stating that a firm called 'Natural Stone Products Ltd' are extracting stone. They are described as 'Quarriers and Suppliers of Dimensional Stone'. Modern-style pictorial warning notices are also displayed by the gate and on fences surrounding the quarry. Although a brief period of quarrying ceased in about 2007, this firm operates as part of the Stirling Stone Group and their website advertises Brownieside sandstone. (Short lengths of rail used as gateposts here are not believed to have come from the Brownieside Quarry railway.) Livestock in the fields can wander unhindered into the quarry.

Currently, the quarry has two faces at approximately 90 degrees to each other. The face lying approximately east-west is about 30 metres in length whilst that lying north-south is about 20 metres in length. These is little overburden to remove. The stone is a durable medium sandstone described by Stirling Stone as having a 'warm pink to purple' colour. It has, apparently, been used for various building applications and it is claimed that it retains sharp masonry detailing even after 100 years of exposure to the elements! Several large blocks rest in the quarry, many bearing painted numbers. A locked container is located just inside the quarry. Outside the quarry entrance there is a man-made level area on the hillside which may have been a loading bank for the former railway. From the side of this a slight hollow leads eastwards for a short distance. The hollow ends by a field-gate at the west end of a conifer plantation. The original trackbed occupied this hollow, or 'cutting', in the hillside, leading eastwards down to the lane by the cottages. When the adjacent moorland was converted to farmland, stones, lifted by the plough, were tipped into the hollow and the land level was raised. Conifers were then planted on this obliterating almost all of the former trackbed except for the slight hollow at the upper end. At the lower (east) end of the trees part of the cutting was filled in to level the ground for a garden for one of the cottages. The trackbed must have deviated slightly to the north here so as to avoid some of the cottage outbuildings. The 'lie of the land' is several metres above the nearby access lane at this point.

The date, probably early in the 20th century, when the railway was constructed, has not yet been discovered. It is believed, however, that it consisted of two parallel tracks, likely of narrow gauge, running approximately east-west in the cutting linking the quarry with 'chutes' at the side of the lane. These chutes were elevated and for the purpose of tipping stone onto road lorries. Each rail line had at least one small tipper wagon with a cable, wound around a braked drum at the quarry end, connecting the wagons on each line. The system thus operated as a gravity-worked self-acting incline, with the descending loaded wagons on one line hauling up the empties on the other.

In a sound recording made some years ago, Belford resident Tom Braidford (born in 1930) remembered seeing remains of the line (pieces of metal and pulley wheels in the cutting) when passing by bus along the A1 from Belford to Alnwick. Bobby Dickson, also of Belford, recalled the railway's cutting still in existence after World War II when he worked nearby. He remembers the curve at its lower end which by-passed the cottages. However, the dates of the line's operation, closure and lifting have not yet been confirmed, and are almost certainly before the years that can be recalled by even the oldest of local residents. One of the nearby cottages has been in the Stewart family for around 80 years. They do not recall their forebears mentioning anything of the railway and consider it unlikely that the cottage would have been purchased if an active railway had been in existence just a few metres away from the property. This may, therefore, date the railway's activities to before the late 1920s.

Chapter Four

The Embleton and Craster Quarry Railways

The whinstone of the 'Whin Sill' has been an excellent source of roadstone as a result of its hard-wearing qualities. Extensive quarries in the areas of Embleton and Craster have extracted this stone and dispatched it nationwide and overseas by road or sea. Both railways and cableways have been involved. Within the last chapter of this volume various other 'proposed' railways in these areas will be described.

12 - The Embleton Quarry Railway

The stone industry at Embleton can be said to have started when a certain Thomas Appleby moved from Barnard Castle to the village in 1840 and established a business as a stone merchant. His son, known as Tom, born in 1847, assisted him and a small quarry was established by 1864. A second son, Mark, born in 1853, entered the business also and the concern traded as 'T. & M. Appleby, Stone Merchants'. They operated from several quarries including one opposite Grey's Inn (a public house in the village), some other small quarries nearby, and in a field by the cottage known as 'Sunny Brae' and referred to as

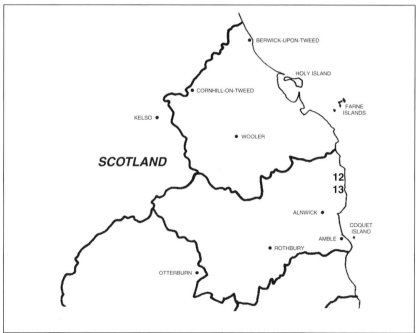

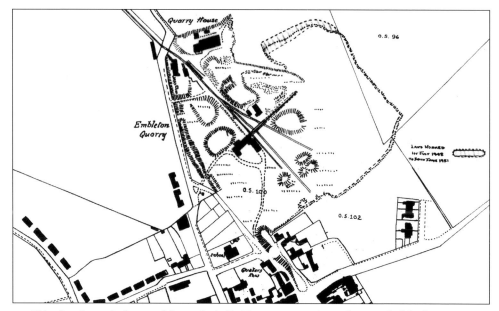

This plan shows the layout of the tracks in Embleton quarry prior to the arrival of the first steam locomotive. Note the absence of any run-round loop, unnecessary when horse-shunting alone was employed. The offices were located in the building marked 'Quarry House'.

Northumberland Record Office

A delightful picture of some of the workers, and local lads, photographed within Embleton Quarry. The Manager, Mark Appleby, is the gentleman wearing the suit with his pocket watch on its chain, third from the left in the back row. *Northumberland Gazette*

the Bleezer Quarries. Finally there was another, which became the largest quarry, at the side of the B1339 road to the north of the village (NU232229). This quarry lies some 6½ miles north-east of Alnwick. When the concern started the land belonged to the Tankerville family but in 1868 it was sold to a Samuel Eyres (sometimes written as 'Ayres') of Leeds. After Eyres' death towards the last years of the 19th century, the land was administered jointly by the Trustees of his Estate and a Mrs Mansell. Later, in 1919, it became the property of Sir Arthur Sutherland, one time Lord Mayor of the City of Newcastle. Finally, after the cessation of quarrying in the 1960s, Alnwick District Council took over the site and used part of the quarry for waste disposal.

The census of 1881 indicates the occupations of men at Embleton. It includes Mark Appleby, living at Grey's Inn with his wife and three daughters, and his brother Thomas ('Tom') living at the Hare & Hounds Inn, with his wife and two sons. Tom is described as a Stone Merchant, employing over 10 sett makers, two stone-breakers, three blacksmiths, several stonemasons and a quarry labourer. The younger brother of Mark and Tom, called William, born 1858, was originally one of the sett makers, but after Tom's death in 1894, he ran the quarry with brother Mark (Tom Appleby, Senior, had died in 1886.) The Applebys had other stone interests at Craster, Belford, Kirkwhelpington and Wooler.

Over 20 men gained a living from the main Embleton quarry, though this number was to increase later. Some of these lodged in a 'lodging house' within the village. The stone was originally carted from the quarry either to Craster harbour or to the station at Christon Bank. It was used for house building, paving, kerbstones, road chippings and setts, later also for making tarmacadam. The distribution of stone by cart continued until the 1890s. It was in the *Contract Journal* of the 27th March, 1895 that a notice appeared inviting tenders for the construction of a tramway from the Embleton Whinstone Quarries to Christon Bank station on the North Eastern Railway's (NER) main line. The notice appeared over the name of William Appleby, described as the quarry foreman. He then lived in Dene View, Embleton.

The arrangements between Eyres and the Applebys for the quarrying of stone appear to have been 'informal' for the 30 years after 1868, for the lease which was drawn up on 12th May, 1898 was described as the 'First Lease'. This lease allowed the Applebys to construct a tramway between the quarry and Christon Bank station. It was to be built with minimum damage to the land over which it passed. The lease empowered the lessees to 'have the right to run wagons and trucks by horse traction over and along the said tramway'. The lease was to be subject to arrangements being made with Sir Edward Grey of the local estate, Northumberland County Council and Alnwick Rural District Council. These bodies had a vested interest in that the tramway was planned to traverse several fields, make three road crossings and to run alongside another road. A plan, with the same date, was attached to the lease. This was drawn by George Reswell, the architect and surveyor, who had offices in Alnwick and Morpeth. The rent would be a 'certain' £200 per annum for quarrying the stone plus a land rent of £12 per annum. In addition there would be a levy of 1s. per cubic yard of stone removed from the quarry. The plan indicated that two sidings would be constructed at Christon Bank yard, one to each side of a standard gauge siding. Gates were to be provided on either side of the Alnwick road at Christon Bank, then two more gates where Station Road (leading to Embleton village) was crossed. Further gates would be provided at field boundaries on the land of North Farm (where a public footpath was crossed). Finally two gates were to be provided where the tramway was to cross the road opposite the quarry and close to Embleton village. The line was to be single throughout apart from a siding in the field opposite North Farm. Two long sidings were shown in the quarry. The total length of the line was just less than 1½ miles. Gradients were unlikely to cause any problem to the horses as there were only small undulations; the surveyed 'spot heights' outside the Blink Bonny and 100 yards along the road from the quarry were identical! Presumably Samuel Eyres must have recently died, for the lease named his Trustees who were Arthur Henry Sharp (of Dumbleton Hall, Gloucestershire), Frederick Charles Marshall (of London), Sir Jacob Wilson (of Chillingham Barns, Belford) and Charles Thomas Eyres (of Grosvenor Square, London). The lease came into effect on 22nd August, 1898, the quarry being described as within a field of 4.9 acres.

The lease specified that horse traction must be used and referred to the line as a tram- or wagon-way. It required the maintenance of all hedges, gates and road crossings. These road crossings were to be properly paved after the track had been laid. The loads in the wagons were prohibited from projecting over the sides of the wagons by more than 1 ft 6 in. The lease allowed both whinstone and freestone to be removed from the quarry for a period of 21 years. Clearly the lease did not meet all requirements for several amended leases were drawn up over the next few years. Another lease, from the trustees of the late Samuel Eyres and Mrs Mansell, was dated 22nd August, 1899, and yet another was dated 3rd October, 1900. This last document involved the lease of stables, horse-keepers' cottages and premises and was to last for 21 years. The rent was to be £50 payable half-yearly, also insurance was required to be arranged and paid for by the Applebys. A further lease was agreed in April 1905 allowing stone to be quarried and transported along the tramway for 21 years, and yet one more was agreed in 1910! This 21-year lease reduced some of the rents payable to a 'certain', or minimum, rent of £50 per annum, a surface rent of £15 per annum and a royalty of 1s. per cubic yard of material removed.

However, by this time dramatic changes had occurred in the mode of operation of the tramway. The first of the two steam locomotives had arrived. This event was to necessitate changes to the track layouts at both the quarry and Christon Bank yard. These changes are recorded on a surviving plan dated 1909. At the Christon Bank terminal the tramway line is shown arriving after crossing the Alnwick road. It split into two soon after passing the gate onto the NER's property. The first line consisted of a siding, parallel to and to the west of two North Eastern Railway sidings. The second line passed onto a loading dock with one NER siding to the east and another siding (leading to the goods shed) to the west. On the loading dock there was a run-round loop allowing the incoming locomotive to run around its train, attach itself to the other end and position the wagons where needed for unloading. A second loop was provided at the quarry end of the tramway allowing the locomotive to run-round the train of empty wagons hauled back from Christon Bank to the quarry.

The first locomotive, which arrived in 1904, was very unusual, being the only locomotive manufactured by Arnold Jung Lokomotivfabrik Gmbh, of Jungenthal bei Kirchen, in Germany, to be bought 'new' for industrial service in Britain. It was a small 2 ft 9 in. gauge 0-4-0 well-tank locomotive with outside cylinders. Its works number was 812 and it carried the name *Dunstanburgh* at Embleton. It was immediately put to work hauling the trains on the tramway and proved to be very satisfactory. However, within a few years the need for a second locomotive arose. Once again the Applebys opted for a German locomotive, very similar to the first. The second locomotive was also an 0-4-0 well tank with outside cylinders but this time built by Orenstein & Koppel in Berlin with works number 3248. It arrived new, from Germany, in 1909 and was allocated the name *Fanny Gray*, after Frances, the wife of Thomas Appleby (senior). Like the first locomotive it was supplied through Arthur Koppel, acting as sales agent. This locomotive was to share the work with *Dunstanburgh* until railway operations ceased at the quarry in 1937 when the quarry temporarily closed. It had been rebuilt by the Hawthorn, Leslie & Co. of Newcastle in 1933 when it was allocated their works number 6438/1933. Both locomotives survived World War II at Embleton without going for scrap. Perhaps it was felt that an upturn in the market for stone would occur after the war and that they might be put back into service. This was not to be and *Dunstanburgh*, largely dismantled by May 1947, was scrapped with *Fanny Gray* in about 1955. (In early 2011 a picture of *Fanny Gray*, in a derelict state within a shed, was advertised for sale on eBay, though the name of the locomotive was incorrectly written as *Franny Gray*. It fetched the princely sum of £24.)

It has been suggested that a third locomotive was present at Embleton, carrying the name *Jotto*. No evidence of this has been found in any of the surviving records related to the quarry and tramway, though one photograph of this locomotive taken in a quarry has been ascribed to Embleton. However, various pieces of evidence in this photograph suggest strongly that this is not correct.

Surviving photographs of the line indicate that steel-sided tipping wagons were in use in the quarry, also some wooden-sided wagons which may have been used for transporting spoil or over-burden. (Horses were used to move wagons within the quarry; in the 1920s these included one named 'Lion' and a former farm horse named 'Punch'.) A smithy at the side of the quarry serviced the machinery and the horses.

In 1910 stone was being moved from Christon Bank to Morpeth and South Shields. Broken whinstone was supplied for the foundations of the Alnwick and Fleetham road. Crushed whinstone was also being transported for the Berwick to Cornhill road just before the start of the Great War. Not all of the stone left via the tramway for, by 1920, Applebys also owned some road vehicles in the form of Sentinel road wagons.

An article in an edition of the *Stone Trades Journal* of 1912 provides an interesting 'snapshot' of Appleby's operations at that time; in addition to the Embleton Quarry he held an additional quarry at Craster:

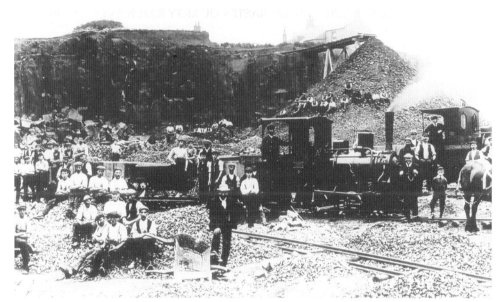

This photograph shows the two Orenstein & Koppel locomotives (with their huge cab front spectacles) inside Embleton Quarry, with at least two sorts of wagon plus a selection of the workforce. *Fanny Gray* is the nearest locomotive. For a time this photograph was sold as a picture postcard.   *Northumberland Gazette*

A second view of the two locomotives, this time apparently double-heading a train of wagons. *Fanny Gray* is the pilot, with *Dunstanburgh* the train engine. Note the differences between the two locomotives: chimney length, cabside handrails and the shape of the cab opening.

Northumberland Gazette

EMBLETON AND CRASTER QUARRIES

These quarries, which are owned by Mr Mark Appleby, were only used to obtain stone for road repairs up to recent times. In view of their favourable position, the business has been opened out for paving setts, channels, road metal, tarmacadam etc. for markets in different parts of Durham and Yorkshire.

Considerable crushing plant by Messrs Ord and Maddison of Darlington has recently been established at both Embleton and Craster, which plant includes the latest patents of the makers for cubical breaking and good screening. The quarries employ from 100 to 120 men and boys.

At Embleton, the stone is taken to the railway station by locomotives and small wagons on a private railway (2' 9" gauge), the distance being 1½ miles. The drilling is done by an 'Ingersoll' steam drill, the usual depth being 20 feet, and all holes are bored from the top, as the stone is in beds, and shoots much better than by breast holes. The crushing and screening plant is driven by a large gas engine, which is worked by suction gas, and all rope haulage and pumping are worked by the same engine. The engine is by Messrs Campbell Gas Engine Company of Halifax, and was installed three years ago, the original being a steam portable engine.

The local term for the crushing and screening plant referred to in this newspaper article was the 'granulator'. The article did not refer to the elevator which raised the rough stone to enter the crushers.

Various reports describe the social conditions of Embleton village in which most of the quarry workers lived. Though the Creighton Memorial Hall, housing a reading room and billiard room for the men, had been opened in the village in October 1903, the village was hardly the attractive place to live in that it is today. A 1911 report refers to the evidence of 'squalor' in the workmen's cottages. Other itinerant quarrymen lived in poor lodging houses, one of these being located near the Sea Lane road junction. However, in the absence of alternative employment, several men lived here and worked at the quarry for most of their working lives. The likely 'record holder' was Thomas Landreth Taylor (shown in the photograph on page 56 as the tall man with a moustache standing next to Mark Appleby). Born in 1857 he started work at the quarry just 10 years later, finally retiring in 1927. After his retirement in 1927 the *Northumberland Gazette* interviewed him and he referred to the Embleton of the mid-19th century as being 'a poor tumble-down place … [and] … one of the roughest villages in Northumberland'. Another employee, weigh clerk Albert Bowden, held the post for 41 years and Jim Blair was the quarry foreman for 38 years.

Despite having a population of just 400 the village had eight public houses! Quarrying was thirsty work but nevertheless drunkenness was common.

Appleby's had become a limited company, called Mark Appleby Ltd, on 29th October, 1913. Father Mark died in 1912 but his son, also Mark, who had learned the stone trade by working in the quarry, was now 28 and running the company with his brother William. 'Young Mark' was to occupy a distinctive position in the community, becoming an alderman later in life.

It is perhaps useful to follow a consignment of stone as it was taken from the quarry to the yard at Christon Bank. After being tipped onto the elevator leading to the crushers and screens, the stone would be raised into the overhead bunkers awaiting the arrival of a train of empty wagons hauled by either *Dunstanburgh* or *Fanny Gray*. The wagons would be loaded and the train would be hauled slowly out

After leaving the quarry the track crossed over the village road before following field sides on its way towards Christon Bank. This is a present-day view taken from the road crossing with the trackbed clearly visible. *Author*

On the section of the line which ran parallel to Station Road, Embleton, the trackbed was raised on a slight embankment, still visible in this 2011 photograph, immediately beyond the fence and trees. *Author*

of the quarry sidings, past the open gates and over the level crossing with the village road. The train would build up speed on its route close to the hedge at the side of the field. Shortly, however, it was necessary for the engine's brakes to be applied for the sharpest of curves to the left opposite North Farm where the direction of the train changed from north-westwards to south-westwards. The siding on the left, a 'store' for spare wagons, was passed without stopping. Just a few yards further on there was more squealing of wheel flanges as the line, following the almost right-angled bend in the adjoining Station Road, once more headed almost north-westwards. On reaching Lambert's Lane it was necessary for a stop for the gates to be opened before the train could emerge onto the section of line where it became an unfenced roadside tramway. (This road crossing is still referred to, by some older residents, as 'Johnny's Crossing' after one of the locomotive drivers, Johnny Thompson.) The milepost ('6 miles to North Sunderland, 8 miles to Alnwick') was then passed as the train gathered speed for the final section towards Christon Bank, already visible ahead. Though the line was without serious gradients there was a short downhill section here, just before the gated Alnwick road-crossing. Here the train passed, on its right, the laundry which had been built by the Greys of Falloden and Howick, as a means of providing some employment for local women. It also performed dry-cleaning and dyeing of cloth. The building's use, as a shop, general store and Post Office for the village, was well in the future! Crossing the Alnwick road and passing through the gates opposite the 'Blink Bonny' hotel and public house, the locomotive worked hard as it entered the yard of the North Eastern Railway and climbed onto the elevated loading bank or 'wharf'. This was raised so as to facilitate the loading of the standard gauge wagons. The loading bank and exchange sidings were located on the opposite side of the level crossing from the Christon Bank station platforms. In North Eastern Railway documents the place of transhipment was known as 'Embleton Quarry Loading Wharf'. After the train had come to a stand in the loop the locomotive was uncoupled ready to run-round the train. The locomotive would then reverse the short distance to the roadside outside the gates where it would take water from the water tank mounted high on a wooden trestle. When the tanks were replenished the locomotive would re-enter the yard. The loaded wagons would be shunted for unloading whilst empties would be marshalled ready to be taken back to the quarry. (No doubt there were occasions when the driver would pop over the road for a 'quick half' at the 'Blink Bonny' before returning with the train of empties to Embleton!)

The importance of the small railway can be judged from the figures indicating that 31,375 tons of stone passed through the exchange sidings at Christon Bank station in 1913 together with 2,407 tons of building stone. In recognition of the revenue which the North Eastern Railway (and later the LNER) derived from transporting the stone, Appleby was provided with a complimentary rail travel pass.

Records exist showing that the Applebys negotiated a new agreement for the lease of the quarry and nearby Glebe Farm in 1917. The lease is dated 25th March of that year. The rental is stated as £124 with a surface rent of £15 16s. 10d. and a minimum stone rent of £10 5s. 0d.

Business was fair throughout the 1920s and 1930s but Mark Appleby made sound decisions to rationalize the business, selling redundant plant and concentrating on the more productive quarries. Old plant was sold from his

This is the entrance for the narrow gauge stone trains into the yard at Christon Bank. Note the signal box on the far side of the Newcastle to Berwick line and the carts in front of the 'Blink Bonny' public house on the right.   *Alan Dixon Collection*

The 'Blink Bonny' public house stands opposite the site of the former exchange sidings at Christon Bank station. The author was surprised to come across this picture postcard of the pub, with, on the right-hand side, next to the tree, one of the Embleton locomotives hauling a train towards the camera! Note the large cab spectacles on the engine.   *Author's Collection*

quarries at Low Newton and Craster, whilst the introduction of a new tarmacadam plant at Embleton opened up a new way of marketing the quarry's stone. To modernize stone distribution Appleby purchased, at the start of the 1930s, four 3-ton, petrol-engined Bedford lorries for local stone deliveries to replace the two Sentinel steam lorries, mentioned earlier, which had previously delivered stone locally. Successfully completed contracts around this time included the supply of stone for the improvements being made to the highway at Waren and for the rebuilding of Waren Mill Bridge (1927), supplying 230 tons of stone per day to Coldstream station when Scott's of Wooler were unable to fulfil a contract (1929) and various other large orders to supply stone for Northumberland County Council. These deliveries were made to various stations in the county, including Glanton where some 1,200 tons of tarmacadam were delivered (also in 1929). Embleton supplied freestone for the repair of the facings of buildings in Edinburgh and whinstone setts for the paving of the roadway approaches to the first Mersey Tunnel. Other north of England cities, including Leeds, used Embleton stone on their roads.

Up to 60 men (including some winter-time casual labourers consisting of local fishermen and also Irishmen) were being employed at this time. However, in the 1930s the number of staff employed at the quarry was reduced to around 40. This total included an office manager, his assistant, a foreman and a clerk. Working in the quarry were about seven labourers, a dozen or so 'knockers up' who broke the stone into suitable sizes for the sett makers, a dozen sett makers and a few tarmac mixers. In addition around half a dozen men were responsible for the road and rail wagons. Finally two blacksmiths and three joiners serviced the quarry equipment. In the 1930s the office manager was a John Fogget, and his assistant was George Smart.

As the 1930s progressed yet more ageing plant was sold including a Robey steam engine (1936), two boilers in scrap condition (1938) and a 50 hp portable engine formerly used in Embleton Quarry (1940).

The quarry's output reached another peak in 1941 when, between the months of May and November, 26,209 tons of stone left the quarry. By this time, of course, the tramway had ceased operation and the stone was taken out by road, much of it to help the war effort. The quarry continued its success story into the 1950s. Between 1951 and 1957 the annual production never fell below 15,000 tons per annum, the maximum production in this period being in 1955 when 19,751 tons left the quarry. However, Appleby had made a forecast back in October 1953 that stone production would have to cease 'within five to ten years' because of faults in the rock. He realised that it would become more uneconomic to work the quarry for, as well as the 'faulting', there were problems associated with the increasing amount of overburden and water drainage from the site. In the event in 1959 he negotiated an extension to his lease of just two years, the quarry producing just over 12,000 tons of stone in 1960 and just under 10,000 in 1961. Another two year extension saw the last blasting take place on 11th January, 1962. The Appleby 'dynasty' at the quarry came to an end when this extension to the lease expired on 11th November, 1963. However, it was to be at least two more years before the final dismantling, demolition or disposal of the machinery and plant items took place. On the closure of the quarry the then company Secretary, George Smart, destroyed all

On entering Christon Bank the stone trains would slow for the crossing of the Alnwick Road, passing, on their right, the premises of the Christon Bank Laundry, whose staff are posed for this early photograph. Note the trackbed in the foreground. The building survives today, albeit housing a shop and post office. *Young Family collection*

The company offices at Embleton Quarry are the only surviving buildings associated with Appleby's enterprise (apart from some cottages in the village where quarrymen resided). These are currently (2011) dangerous to enter and warning notices advertise their near-dereliction. *Author*

Another German locomotive, *Jotto*, may have worked at Embleton, though the author has found no documentary evidence of this. However, it appears in the Industrial Locomotive Society's list of named locomotives ascribed to 'Mark Appleby' and its photograph appeared in the archive of an Alnwick photographer along with photographs of the Embleton locomotives.   *Murphy Family Collection*

of the office records including records of staff wages, sales and deliveries. (This has made the putting-together of the quarry history a more difficult task!)

The quarry ultimately came under the ownership of Alnwick District Council. There have been various council plans for the site, including the building of a small development of houses. Unfortunately the site has not been fully 'degassed' following its short-term use as a tip for Alnwick's rubbish and hence no housing development has taken place. Other plans for the site have included its development as a wildlife area with lake, with just a few houses to be built on the west side. Plans in 1988 to transform the quarry into a leisure area came to naught. At the present time the quarry is used by Embleton's residents for walking their dogs. A pleasant walk can be enjoyed around the east side of the quarry where its lower levels have become a lake frequented by waterfowl and seabirds. There is a fine view towards Dunstanburgh Castle to the south-east. The village recycling bins are located in the lay-by near to the quarry entrance.

On the north side 'Quarry House' survives in a derelict state. Notices mounted on the walls by the council identify the hazard and warn against unauthorized entry. No identifiable traces remain in the quarry of the workshops of the craftsmen, the rail lines, or of the crushing and loading structures, though debris abounds. However, the route of the railway, with its sharp curves, is easily followed along the sides of the fields near to, and alongside Station Road, and the wide grassy verge at the side of the road as it approaches Christon Bank indicates the former tramway alignment. The former laundry building and the 'Blink Bonny' are still present (the latter as a popular pub and restaurant) but a recent housing development now occupies the site of the former station yard. Though the station closed on the 15th September, 1958 many of its 150-years-old durable stone buildings survive, converted into dwellings. Several of the public houses, used by the workmen, survive in Embleton village. Some have decorated their walls with copies of photographs of the former quarries and tramway. In 1953 some cine film was taken of activities at Embleton Quarry and members of the now-defunct Embleton Local History Society recall it being shown at a meeting in 1990.

Christon Bank may have had another small line of rails, for, just off the Alnwick road, is a cart track leading to an old limeworks dating back to the first half of the 19th century. The two kilns, forming Christon Bank Limeworks, obtained their limestone from the adjacent quarry and coal, either from a small pit located between the Alnwick road and the East Coast main line, or from a pit located just to the south-west of the kilns. The lime produced was used for agricultural purposes. The kilns are now a Grade 2 listed building and the former quarry, now filled with water and stocked with fish, has been used, even by Earl Grey, as a pond for angling purposes. It has been suggested by some local residents that a small tramway was formerly used for loading the tops of the kilns with coal and limestone and for taking the roasted lime away from their bases. Some gently curving earthworks forming a small embankment, now partially obscured by the recent planting of trees, may be remains of this early line. Public paths and tracks lead to the kilns from the adjacent roads. However, no documentary evidence, maps or plans have been found which would confirm the existence of this line.

13 – The Craster Quarry Railways and Cableway

The approach to Craster village and harbour by road presents an unusual sight to visitors: cliff faces which face inland! These cliffs are derived from a huge length of whinstone, various sections of which have been quarried at different times. Quarrying for local purposes took place early in the 19th century from several small quarries near to the village. The first commercial quarry was probably Scotchman's Quarry located to the south of the road as the road approaches the village (NU 255196). This quarry was in use from the mid- to late-19th century. Some of its stone was carted to Craster harbour and then exported by sea. The second quarry to be developed was at Hare's Nick to the north of the road to the village (NU 254198). This operated briefly in the early 20th century and may have used a small tramway or railway. The main quarrying activities took place at Craster Quarry, located on the south side of the road into the village, to the east of the original Scotchmen's Quarry (NU 256197). This quarry was opened in the first years of the 20th century, enjoyed some 'boom years' before the start of World War I, but then fell into decline and closed in the 1920s. There were several brief reopenings before it finally closed in the 1940s. It is this last quarry which provides much of the local railway history in the form of its narrow gauge railway, its craneway and overhead cableway (usually referred to as the 'aerial ropeway').

Some parts of the Northumberland coastline provide little refuge for vessels in times of storm. The original 1891 plans for Craster harbour, drawn up by Mr J. Watt Sandeman, a respected civil engineer with expertise in waterways, envisaged a harbour, both as a place of refuge and as a means of shipping the stone from the quarries on the Dunstanburgh Estate. He considered that the profits from the stone would make the project remunerative. His plans involved two alternatives: the first (the more expensive at £39,000) would involve the construction of a 900 ft northern breakwater with two angled piers at the harbour with an opening between them of 80 ft, with 12 ft of water being present at high tide. The piers would be about 700 ft in length. The second alternative (the cheaper at £28,000) would involve the building of just two simple jetties at the harbour. He anticipated that the dues from shipping could amount to £300-£400 per annum. This scheme was not proceeded with.

Despite the poor harbour facilities some quarrying continued and, according to the *Stone Trades Journal* 'the stone has, so far, been conveyed to the coast by carts, as the distance is less than 100 yards, and the harbour at present most suited to cart traffic…'.

It was a local Craster man, James Roland McLaren, who embarked upon a scheme to improve the harbour facilities, though the early works were paid for by Thomas William Craster of nearby Craster Tower. Parliamentary sanction was obtained in 1905 and in the same year a start was made. By 1906 the first concrete had been laid on one of the piers. This was made from Portland Cement (one part), sand (two parts) and crushed whinstone (three parts), all being sourced locally. By 1907 the north pier was finished. This was 170 ft in length. In October 1908 it was reported that it was hoped to finish the south pier 'shortly'; in fact because of problems this was not completed until the summer of 1910. The south pier was 314 ft in length of which 190 ft would be available for the loading of vessels. Excavations to deepen the harbour were performed by Messrs Brims & Co., the 'penultimate stages' of which were still being executed in May 1909, though some shipments of stone from the quarry had been made by this time. The depth at the harbour entrance was 14 ft 6 in. at spring tides and 11 ft 6 in. at neap tides, the entrance being 50 ft wide at low water. The total harbour area was quoted as 1.75 acres. The quarry's 'official opening' appears to have been in August 1909 and was reported in local newspapers:

A new quarry has just been opened (August 1909) at South Craster and already numerous cargoes of whinstone have been despatched by sea to Goole and Sunderland. The quality of stone is extremely good. There is an abundance of almost unworked whinstone (basalt) in close proximity to the Harbour and preparations are being made for establishing a shipping trade in this community. Stones, rough and paving, can be shipped to various places at reasonable rates.

The tonnage duties for all stone were 4*d*. per ton.

Until this time the quarries, and the accompanying harbour construction, had been entirely under McLaren's supervision. However, in 1910 he entered into discussions with Henry Gordon Prowde, BSc, of St Bede's Terrace, Sunderland, with the aim of forming a partnership to further the development of the stone quarries at Craster. Prowde already had a 'presence' in Northumberland as he was, at that time, the lessee of the quarries at Longhoughton near Alnwick. Together they established a company to be called Craster Whinstone Quarries with a registered office at 15 Pilgrim Street (later removed to 90 Pilgrim Street), Newcastle-upon-Tyne. The share capital was £5,000 of which McLaren subscribed £1,000 and Prowde £1,350, with the balance coming from their families. The company was

A row of steam herring drifters approaches the harbour at Craster whilst a stone boat appears to be standing by outside the harbour, perhaps waiting to follow the drifters into the harbour for loading at the hoppers.   *Commercial postcard. Author's collection*

The SS *Guardian* is tied up next to the stone hopper at the entrance to the harbour at Craster. It appears to be high in the water and awaiting its cargo of stone. Judging by the well-dressed persons watching this would seem to be a special occasion though this event is not recorded on the picture postcard from which this photograph is reproduced.   *Author's Collection*

formally registered with the payment of the necessary fees on 22nd March, 1911. It generally traded under the name McLaren and Prowde Ltd, though this was not an official company registered with Companies House. It was anticipated that between 20,000 and 100,000 tons of stone could be shipped annually with a 42 year supply being available for quarrying. The company was registered for quarrying, stone dressing, sett making and cement manufacture. In 1911 they were advertising for stone workers, masons and men for concrete work.

Rapid developments occurred at the quarries and harbour. By 1911 rails had already been laid in the quarry and wagons were used for moving stone from the quarry faces. A temporary tramway ('tramline' in documents) was laid between the inner harbour and the crushing plant, newly installed at the quarry entrance. This was to facilitate the movement of the final harbour-building materials. Stacks for stone and other material were formed adjacent to the harbour. Plans were instigated for the conveyance of crushed stone from the quarry entrance to the harbour by means of an overhead cableway. At the harbour, loading bins, to facilitate the transfer of whinstone to vessels, were constructed on the south pier. These were completed on 15th June, 1912 and brought into use when the aerial ropeway was fully operational in July 1912. They were to prove to be an excellent investment! They were of 1,000 tons capacity. They formed three elliptical wells, the section of each being 16 ft x 10 ft and with a depth of 50 ft. They were constructed of vertical timber shuttering supported against the horizontal pressure of stone by a number of hoops of flat steel bar. Each was strongly braced to resist wind pressure. The bins were mounted on a reinforced concrete bridge spanning the pier head. The level of the discharge doors was set at 23 ft above the high water of ordinary spring tides. Stone would be discharged from them into the holds of steamers (of up to 1,000 tons) alongside.

Before they were built there were often three vessels loading in the harbour at one time. After installation of the bins, loading of a larger vessel could take between one and two hours, with a vessel needing to be at the harbour for 24 hours at most. Loading occurred at flood tide when there was a minimum of 11 ft of water on the inside face of the quay and 14 ft on the outside. Vessels known to have been involved in the Craster stone trade include the SS *Gertrude, Florence, Clunie, Rhoda, Nero, Millington, Lythe, Latchford, Swin, Ruby, Magilar, Maggy Purves, Cape York, Deansgate, Skinner, Kelpie, Wharfedale, Slateford, Gleno, Dunleith, Guardian* and *Zephyr*. Later the company owned its own vessels the SS *Whinstone* and *Sweet Home*. (Some of these also visited Budle Bay to collect stone.) Destinations for the stone included Whitstable, Rochester, Grimsby, Boston, Hull, Middlesbrough and Goole. In practice loads were of between 100 tons and 600 tons per vessel. Occasionally tug-hauled barges would also load at Craster. Loading was a very dusty process and was very unpopular with the locals especially when it was windy!

It was on 17th June, 1911 that McLaren and Prowde submitted their plans to Alnwick Rural District Council for the construction of an aerial ropeway. The *Alnwick Journal* of that date reported:

AERIAL ROPEWAY CROSSING AT CRASTER
A communication from Messrs McLaren and Prowde, contractors, Craster, enclosed a plan (to the Highways Dept) of an aerial ropeway crossing the Rural District Road in

AERIAL ROPEWAY CROSSING AT CRASTER.

A communication from Messrs McLaren and Prowde, contractors, Craster, enclosed a plan of an aerial ropeway crossing the Rural District Road in Craster which they proposed to erect for the carriage of stone from their quarry and crusher to the harbour. The scheme had been submitted to Mr Craster, who had no objection to it, and considered it would relieve the harbour of a good deal of congestion and interference with the fishermen, and the Council's road from a great deal of wear. There would be no obstruction to the movement of boats. It was proposed to protect the road by a higher guard against the possibility of stone falling from the carriers. The two towers had been placed rather farther apart than was contemplated in order to meet the views of the fishermen, and as a result the length separating them had become rather long —over 50 feet—for a timber guard. Therefore a guard of fine mesh wire netting would be depressed in the centre and stretched from tower to tower over a width of 24 feet. They were anxious to get authority to carry the ropeway across the road at the earliest possible date.

Left: This newspaper cutting from the contemporary local newspaper shows the opening paragraph of the report of the plans of McLaren and Prowde to seek permission to construct the 'aerial ropeway', actually a cableway with suspended hoppers, from the stone crushers at the entrance to Craster Quarry to new hoppers to be constructed on the quay wall.

Northumberland Gazette

Below: This plan shows the possible alternative route for the overhead cableway to a new harbour to be constructed at Muckle Carr. This would have involved building new breakwaters and a specialist stone quay. In the event, perhaps on the grounds of cost, this alternative was not proceeded with.

Northumberland Record Office

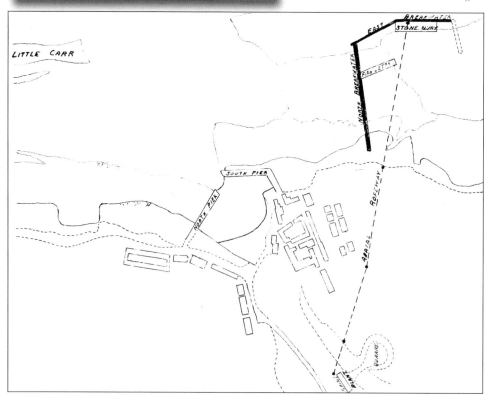

Craster which they proposed to erect for the carriage of stone from their quarry and crusher to the harbour. The scheme had been submitted to Mr Craster, who had no objection to it, and considered it would relieve the harbour of a good deal of congestion and interference with the fishermen, and the Council's road from a great deal of wear. There would be no obstruction to the movement of boats. It was proposed to protect the road by a higher guard against the possibility of the falling of stone falling from the carriers. The two towers had been placed rather further apart than was contemplated in order to meet the views of the fishermen, and as a result, the length separating them had become rather long -over 50 feet- for a timber guard. Therefore a guard of fine mesh netting would be depressed in the centre and stretched from tower to tower over a width of 24 feet. They were anxious to get authority to carry the ropeway across the road at the earliest possible date.

A letter from T.W. Craster, Craster Tower, stated with reference to the proposed aerial ropeway, it appeared that if carried out, this method of conveying the stone would be of benefit by enabling ships to take on board cargoes of stone very quickly, thus leaving the piers free for the herring trade. All the present heavy carting of stone over the road from quarry to harbour would be avoided, thus reducing the cost of repairs over this part of the road very considerably. The standards for the ropeway would be so placed as not to interfere with the other interests concerned, and the Council, if they gave permission for the crossing of the highway, would see that proper precautions were taken to prevent any danger to persons using the road. The quarrying industry promised to become an important one at Craster and anything which would assist its development was worthy of encouragement.

[The reply:] The Clerk: They can go on with it at once unless they interfere with the public right of way. Mr Dixon said there should be some stipulation with regard to the strength of the ropeway over the roadway.

McLaren and Prowde agreed to certain stipulations as regards the strength of the cable and the erection of the protective netting beneath it. Consequently the council agreed to the operation of the aerial ropeway. The building of the aerial ropeway was reported in *The Times* newspaper of 20th March, 1913 which included news of its sanctioning by the Board of Trade:

A scheme for improving the facilities for loading stone at Craster, Northumberland … has been sanctioned by the Board of Trade.

The new loading plant will consist of an aerial ropeway to transport the roadstone from the quarries to the south pier head … into storage bins of about 1,000 tons capacity.

The ropeway is being constructed by Messrs J.M. Henderson and Co., of Aberdeen, and the storage bins have been designed by Mr A.H. Clark of Messrs. McLaren and Prowde (Limited) of Newcastle-on-Tyne, the lessees of Craster Whinstone Quarries.

A surviving plan held in the Northumberland Record Office indicates that there were two routes considered for the aerial ropeway. The route actually constructed linked the crushers at the entrance to the quarry with the hoppers on the South Pier. An alternative route, linking the crushers with a 'Stone Quay' on a proposed new East Breakwater at Muckle Carr was not proceeded with.

Around this time an inventory of plant and equipment was drawn up. Unfortunately it is not dated. However, it indicates that in the quarry there was the company's Foden steam wagon (for local deliveries of stone by road), a 14 hp Ruston Proctor portable engine, a 3-ton 'Smith Bros' steam crane, 2 steam rock drills (and associated items), an unspecified amount of rails and wagons, a Scotch derrick crane [sic], a stone crusher, the crushing mill, an elevator and screens, a gas engine house, an explosives house, a weighbridge and house, a 'concrete mixer or tarmacadam plant' [sic] and a 'ten tone bogie' [sic]. In addition there were other temporary wooden buildings and sheds, plus various carts and horses.

For the first few years business seems to have been brisk. Shipping records, for July 1913 for example, show that seven different vessels loaded at Craster, with the *Cape York* alone taking away a total of 2,000 tons that month. Occasionally two vessels would be loaded at once: in May 1914 the *Ruby* loaded with 200 tons of Macadam and setts whilst simultaneously the *Kelpie* was loaded with 600 tons of roadstone.

However, the onset of war appears to have restricted the stone trade and, partly because of bad weather, just one consignment left in December 1915 and none at all in March 1916. The stone that had been quarried was being stockpiled ready for future collection. However, shortly afterwards, McLaren and Prowde's own steamer left with a cargo of stone for Hull, and plans were made to run a weekly boat between Craster and the Humberside port.

It was in 1917 that Prowde formed his company entitled H.G. Prowde Ltd, for pursuing other quarry interests on his own, though continuing to work with McLaren at Craster.

From the 'one hundred men' employed in the early days of the quarry the number fell to just 17 by 1922. There was one small development on the quarry's internal rail system in the 1920s when a small four-wheeled locomotive, with mechanical transmission, was obtained for the shunting of wagons. It is not known whether this machine was fitted with a petrol engine or diesel engine (the former is, perhaps, more likely), nor has the name of the manufacturer or supplier been discovered. The machine was remembered by a quarryman, the late Jimmy Turnbull, who started his career at Craster in the 1920s before moving to Howick Quarry early in the 1930s. He recalled that it was similar to the one employed at Howick (a small Lister). No shed was provided to house it and it was refuelled and serviced in the open air. The subsequent fate of the locomotive is not known. It moved small 'V-shaped skips' around the quarry.

The quarry closed for the first time in the early 1930s, though it reopened briefly on several occasions. In 1934 *Kelly's Directory* identifies Crow, Catchpole & Co. as operating the Craster Quarry. Around this time the tarmacadam plant was converted to being run with a diesel engine. Originally the quarry had used tar obtained from a coke-works near Newcastle, but by the 1930s bitumen was used.

The quarry closed again but once again reopened under a firm called Kings & Co. of Glasgow. The final demand for stone from the quarry came during World War II when aerodromes were being built for the RAF at nearby Brunton and Boulmer. The former had concrete runways and Craster stone was used in their construction. To alleviate the shortage of labour use was made of Italian prisoners-of-war at the quarry. Final closure of the quarry took place at the end of the war. Subsequently, after the removal of quarry plant, part of the quarry was used as a garden nursery and today it forms a public car park for the village and harbour. The local tourist information centre has been installed in a new building close to the quarry entrance. Remains of the overhead ropeway have disappeared and only the base of the hoppers remains on the south pier, the remainder of the edifice having been taken down, rather than blown up.

Chapter Five

Some Quarry Railways around Alnwick

There were two major quarries at Little Mill, near Littlehoughton, some 3½ miles north-east of Alnwick. To the east of the main line railway was Little Mill Whinstone Quarry (occasionally called Little Mill Quarries North), whilst to the west of the line was Little Mill Limestone Quarry. The limestone quarry and its railway will be described in the next volume. Both had sidings and connections to the main line and operated their own internal narrow gauge tramways. Their histories are closely interlinked, as, at times, they were leased by the same companies or individuals. The whinstone quarry and railway were the first to be closed. Other substantial quarries were worked, with the aid of rail systems, at nearby Howick (which also had sidings with a main-line connection) and to the west of Longhoughton village.

14 - The Little Mill Whinstone Quarry Railway

The Little Mill Whinstone Quarry (NU230175) was created on the land of Little Mill Farm, the farm buildings being located to the north of the quarry site. Work at the quarry did not start until after 12th May, 1865 when the land was leased to a certain William Barkus. Barkus, at that time, was also the lessee of the limestone quarry and lime works on the opposite side of the railway and had other quarry interests at Gunnerton and Greenhead within Northumberland. It is said that he held the 'goodwill' of Ratcheugh Quarry, Longhoughton as well.

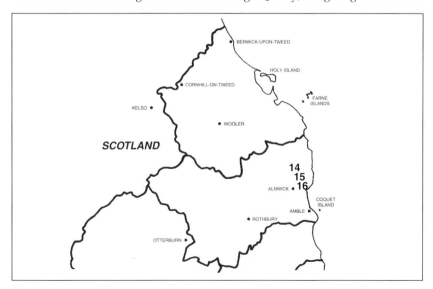

This is an early photograph taken at Little Mill Quarry showing the quarry workers with the quarry lessee, John Richardson, fourth from the left in the second row, wearing a bowler hat.

Author's Collection

These are copies of documents to compare the track layout of the main line whinstone sidings at Little Mill in 1906 with the layout in 1896 at the time of Richardson's assumption of the quarry lease.

Author

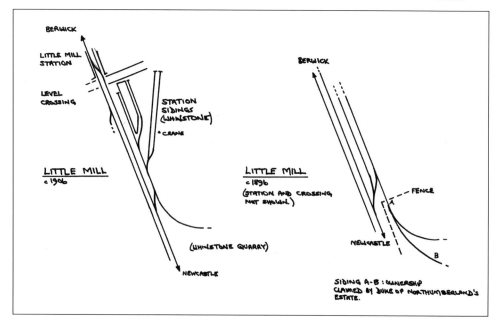

He was a mining engineer by profession. Barkus employed several labourers at Little Mill but his tenancy of the operating quarry was to be rather brief. By 1876 he was clearly in some difficulty financially and decided to assign his interests in the quarry to the Northumberland Whinstone Co. Two years later his business interests failed completely.

The Northumberland Whinstone Co. Ltd had its registered office at 28 Clayton Street West, in Newcastle. This company leased and operated the Little Mill Quarry for almost 20 years. Elsewhere, they operated out of Barrasford, Greenhead and Longhoughton Quarries for over 80 years. Its manager at Little Mill was John Lamb.

In 1895 they declined to pay the increase in rent asked for by the Howick estates and they were issued with a notice to quit, the notice being dated 9th April of that year and signed by George Grey, the estate's valuer and land agent. The tenancy was offered to John H. Richardson, already operating the lime works and quarry opposite and he accepted it. The Whinstone company wrote to Richardson in early 1896:

> We understand that you have taken the Little Mill Whinstone Quarry from May next. We shall be glad to know what plant, if any, you are prepared to take off the hands of the Company and at the Quarry.

Correspondence took place between Richardson and the company regarding the arrangements for Richardson assuming possession. Various receipts survive showing that Richardson purchased some of the quarry machinery in April and May 1896. Within the quarry the company had been operating a tramway system, actually the property of the Howick Estates, and the estate wrote to Richardson asking if he would purchase this. Richardson agreed and the sum of £15 was paid (though his initial offer appears to have been £10). An initial Agreement between Richardson and the estate was made and this allowed him to continue with the quarrying of stone, though the first formal Lease document was dated 12th May, 1902. This permitted Richardson to quarry 6,000 tons of stone per year, in return for an annual rent of £125, with a royalty of 6*d.* per ton for dressed stone and 3*d.* per ton for rough stone to be paid. At the end of the lease the landlord, the Howick estates, would have the right to purchase any of the quarry plant.

Did Richardson take on a sound business?

Mr Lamb, on behalf of the Whinstone company had been asking for a rent reduction on the grounds that the quarry was making a profit of only £60 annually, exclusive of management charges. However, Richardson certainly took over, at little cost, a quarry that was certainly well equipped with plant. An Inventory dating from around the time of Richardson's take-over of the lease shows that the quarry contained a smith's shop, an engine house, a powder magazine, a 'cart weigh and weigh house', a 'tram weigh and weigh house' [*sic*], a boiler house, a second engine house, a stonebreakers' house and an old boiler used as a water tank. In addition there was an extensive system of narrow gauge tramway lines and tubs, plus some standard gauge sidings which linked with the main line.

The quarry had certainly been producing good quantities of stone. In the early years of the Northumberland Whinstone Company's occupancy between

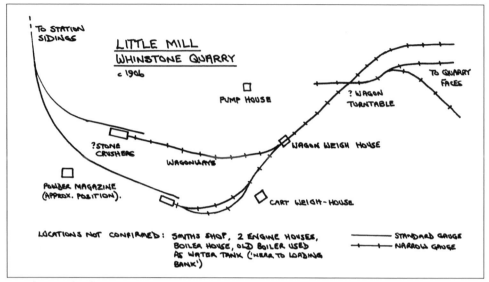

This is a sketch, not drawn to scale, compiled from various sources which shows the layout of some of the quarry plant and both standard and narrow gauge lines in Little Mill Quarry in 1906. The narrow gauge lines were, of course, regularly moved to new quarry faces.   *Author*

This April 1941 photograph shows Manning, Wardle locomotive *Despatch* (Works No. 1230), built in 1892, at Little Mill Quarry. By this date it was possibly out of use, though it was known to have been working some five years earlier.   *Beamish Museum Collection*

3,000-4,000 tons of stone were quarried annually. The quantity peaked at 8,764 tons in the year 1885-86 but settled down at around 6,000 tons per year. In the last year of their operation, when they only operated for just over half of the months, the total fell to just under 4,000 tons. On Richardson's take-over he expanded the quarry size by opening new faces and extending the quarry in a north-easterly direction in 1896, and towards the south-east in 1897. The total of stone production rose initially to an average of about 8,000 tons per year but then, in the first years of the 20th century, there was a rapid increase. By 1903 the annual total reached 10,280 tons, then 14,802 in 1906. These totals included all of the stone sold, that is, kerbs, setts, roadstone and rubble. The peak was reached in 1913 when the North Eastern Railway's records indicate that 12,678 tons of roadstone were shipped from the sidings at Little Mill station together with 8,443 tons of building stone, just over 21,000 tons in total. This figure might have included some stockpiled stone, as Richardson's own records indicate that only 18,213 tons were quarried that year. Alternatively some other stone from, for example, Craster Quarry, may have been loaded onto main line wagons here.

After a slight downturn at the start of the Great War, trade improved and an advertisement in the *Berwick Advertiser* of 24th August, 1917 read: 'Quarrymen, stonebreakers and a good engine driver wanted. Apply at Little Mill Quarries North.'

A staff list, dated May 1925 shows that the workforce was made up of two foremen, two enginemen, five quarrymen, 14 labourers, one blacksmith, seven sett makers and eight stone breakers, The quarry was, at this time, working six days per week. By 1929 a similar list indicates the employment of two foremen, two enginemen, seven quarrymen, 10 labourers, seven sett makers, two kerb dressers and one stone breaker.

The sidings at Little Mill were listed in the *Handbook of Stations* for the early years of the 20th century. However, as well as sending out stone by rail towards the south, Richardson was also supplying stone locally. Customers included the Ashington Urban District Council who received many tons of 6 in. x 3 in. setts for use in a road improvement programme. Lesbury village roads and the nearby Alnmouth Road were improved using 801 yards of 12 in. x 6 in. chisel-dressed whinstone kerbs supplied from Little Mill. Deliveries were also made to the County Council. Trade held up in the 1920s but the onset of the 1930s saw a decline in the demand for dressed stone. From a 1935 total of 2,243 tons of dressed stone sold, the figures fell to 577 tons in 1937, 153 tons in 1940 and none at all in 1941 and 1942. The sales of rough stone held up for slightly longer. In 1940, a good year, some 8,022 tons were sold but this dropped to under 6,000 by 1943. By 1948 the tonnage had fallen to 1,738 and in the next year, the final full year of quarry operations, just 952 tons were sold.

On 13th October, 1948 Henry ('Harry') Richardson, son of the now elderly John, reported to the Howick Estates that he had received a letter from Messrs Trollope & Colls expressing an interest in the quarry. Earl Grey, on behalf of the Howick estates, wrote to the company and asked them to confirm their interest. On 7th March, 1949 they indicated that they were willing to lease the quarry. They had inspected the plant and machinery still being used by the Richardsons

This photograph of *Despatch*, though undated, was probably taken around the same time as the previous one. The shine on the cylinder covers and the smokebox is more likely as a result of a recent shower of rain rather than any attempt to clean the locomotive for the photograph!

Beamish Museum Collection

This photograph shows the interior of part of the cab of *Despatch*. Even after several years of being out-of-use, some of the cab fittings, the works plate and nameplates remain attached to the locomotive. One nameplate survives, today, in private ownership. The identity of the private owner wagon 5-plank wagon has not been confirmed.

J.W.Armstrong Trust

but pronounced that it was largely old and small-scale. They did, however, express a desire to purchase a pump, the tramway and a weighbridge, but not the rest. The negotiated lease was to start on 12th May, 1949. However, on 17th April, 1950 Trollope & Colls found it necessary to question how matters were proceeding: 'It is getting on for a year since we took over the quarry in May 1949 and we have not received a copy of the Lease document'.

This stimulated the Howick Estates into some action and the document was finally sent, having been signed and sealed on 12th October, 1950. No records survive in the Howick Estate records as to how long the Trollope & Colls lease lasted or whether they quarried any stone at Little Mill. Trollope & Colls have since that time undergone several takeovers, first to the Trafalgar Group, then to the Kvaerner Group and, not unsurprisingly, it has not been possible to trace any of their archive material related to Little Mill!

There were two facets of railway operations at Little Mill Whinstone Quarry: firstly the narrow gauge tramway within the quarry and secondly the standard gauge operations in the sidings connected to the main line.

Fortunately a plan, dating from around 1900, survives showing the tramway system within the quarry, backed up by visual evidence from one surviving photograph. This photograph shows several wooden-bodied side-tipper wagons, tracks and a wagon turntable where two tracks crossed. The 2 ft 6 in. gauge tramway served the various quarry faces and stone was led to a weighbridge where the contents of individual wagons could be weighed; the men's earnings depended on the weight of stone they had loaded. Stone was then transferred to hoppers ready for loading into standard gauge wagons. In the early days manpower was used to shift the wagons, though later horses were used. An outline of the tramway system is also shown on the Ordnance Survey maps surveyed in the 1920s.

The standard gauge rail system within the quarry gates consisted of a long siding, just over 161 yards in length which ran to the stone loading point. This was part of the quarry property. Close to the gate there was another siding, just over 46 yards in length which remained the property of Earl Grey even after the track within the quarry had been sold to Richardson. These two lines joined and ran towards a loading bank to the north side of the road level crossing. One siding was located on each side of this bank. In addition, towards the eastern side of the yard, there was one, later two, long sidings for the storage of wagons: 'fulls' ready to be taken away up the main line by the pick-up goods, and 'empties' awaiting movement into the quarry for loading. A trailing connection from the up main line led to the Little Mill sidings. Although there was a trailing connection between the up and down main lines the whinstone sidings were normally served by trains heading southwards. The main line connections to both the whinstone and limestone quarries at Little Mill were removed in the late 1960s.

Two small steam locomotives are known to have shunted the private sidings at Little Mill Whinstone Quarry. Unfortunately the precise dates of their operation are not known. The first locomotive, which may have carried 'No. 6', was an 0-4-0 well tank engine, with outside cylinders measuring 10 in. x 20 in. The number must have been that carried in previous ownership, perhaps in Cumberland. It was built by the manufacturers Fletcher Jennings at their Lowca Works in Whitehaven, Cumbria. Its works number and year of construction are

These are the remains of the former weigh-house for road lorries at Little Mill sidings adjacent to the East Coast main line. Once again the photograph was taken from the adjacent level crossing with the barriers raised. *Author*

This is a present day photograph of the Little Mill whinstone quarry showing some of the former stone faces. The quarry is now flooded, and, as it lies on a private estate, it forms a peaceful haven for wildlife. Various species of birds both feed from the lake and nest on the surrounding cliffs. *Author*

not known. Whilst at Little Mill it received some repairs and had a new firebox fitted by a concern called Thomas Black & Sons of Tweedmouth; this firm is better known as a manufacturer of spades! After use at Little Mill it may have passed into the ownership of Chirnside Paper Mills, or, alternatively, it may have been dismantled and scrapped rather than resold, according to which source is to be believed. It has been suggested that a boiler used for storing water at the quarry in later years came from this locomotive.

A little more is known about the replacement locomotive which arrived second-hand from Messrs Carr & Co. of Carlisle, via dealer Thomas Ward, to take over the work from the Fletcher Jennings locomotive. It was an 0-4-0 well and saddle tank, also with outside cylinders, built by Manning, Wardle & Co. Ltd, at Hunslet in Leeds in 1892 and carried the name *Despatch*. In 1924 Carr's had bought a fireless locomotive to replace this Manning, Wardle as locomotives of this type posed less of a fire risk in their biscuit works. A photograph of the new fireless *Despatch* at Carr's appeared in the *Carlisle Journal* in March 1925. This suggests that the transfer of the original *Despatch* to the north-east was in the middle years of the 1920s. Its works number was MW 1230 and it still carried the *Despatch* nameplates on its side tanks at Little Mill, though the *Carlisle Journal* stated that the name was 'transferred to the fireless one'.

It is known that *Despatch* was still at work at Little Mill in 1936 though on less-busy days the shunting was performed by a heavy horse. After years of service it spent some years derelict in the closed quarry before being scrapped. One of its brass nameplates, showing the name in brass against a red background, survives in preservation. Fortunately several photographs of the locomotive, taken at the end of its working life, or when derelict in the quarry, have survived. It was scrapped in the early 1950s, probably in February 1951. It is not known whether the Little Mill locomotives, normally based in the whinstone quarry were permitted to cross over to the limestone quarry sidings when shunting was required there. The North Eastern *Appendices to the Rule Book and Working Timetables* for the period beginning 1st March, 1922, perhaps surprisingly, contain nothing about the movement of private locomotives over NER tracks. The section of the appendix which lists specific instructions for individual locations contains no reference to Little Mill. The trailing crossover, mentioned earlier and located adjacent to the signal box and level crossing, would have made a transfer of a locomotive between the quarries possible. However it is likely that the Richardson locomotive was confined to the sidings in the Whinstone Quarry, the main line company's locomotives off the pick-up goods trains performing other shunting as required. There is no mention, in the surviving records, of any standard gauge private-owner wagons belonging to the quarry lessees. It is very likely that wagons of the main line companies were used to remove the stone.

Today the quarry lies on private land. Access, only with permission from the landowner, is possible from a track, which was constructed in the 1970s, from the nearby main road. Inside the new quarry gate there is a flat grassy area which is sometimes used by anglers as a car park. Today the quarry, which, in its working days was sometimes a 'wet' quarry and necessitated the operation of a water pump, includes a small lake used by waterfowl. The quarry faces are prominent and are used by birds, especially seabirds, for nesting. Few remains exist to show that sidings and loading bank existed at this site, the remains of the weigh-house and some traces of fencing being all that survive. Little Mill station was closed and demolished many years ago, though the adjacent level crossing, albeit with modern automatic barriers and synthetic roadway, survives. Crossovers still link the two running lines at this point which are signalled for bi-directional running.

15 - *The Howick Quarry Railway*

Howick Quarry (NU237168), sometimes referred to as Howick Heugh Quarry, was opened as a source of whinstone in the early years of the 20th century. The quarry is located at Hough (or Heugh) Hill, west of the road leading from Longhoughton to Embleton, now the B1339. Its first lessee was John Richardson who also operated the whinstone quarry and limestone quarry at Little Mill, less than a mile away to the north-west. He had removed very little stone and the quarry was very small at the start of the 1920s.

In 1921 the quarry became leased, by the Howick Estate, to Ernest Robinson Metcalf of Littlehoughton, who entered into a partnership with Henry Richardson of Sunderland (was this John's son?). Together they formed a company to be known as Howick Whinstone Company Ltd. Their scheme involved the quarrying of whinstone from Hough Hill and it was planned to produce both roadstone and setts (to include kerbstones) at the quarry. It would be transported by means of a siding connection with the adjacent main line. Their lease involved using 1.959 acres of land, which had formerly been part of the adjacent farm, leased by a Mr Glahome. Negotiations were entered into with the North Eastern Railway and an agreement was reached on 14th October, 1921. The NER was to build the sidings and the main line link, but the cost would be met by Metcalf. A start on the works was made soon after the Agreement was signed and they were opened shortly afterwards. The sidings were located about one mile south of Little Mill crossing and 1½ miles north of Longhoughton station.

Problems arose soon after the completion of the sidings and the main line link! Farmer Glahome complained to the Howick Estates, the lessors, that sheep had escaped from his farmland onto the siding and also the main line railway as the fencing was inadequate. Howick Whinstone Company's reply was that the lines were correctly fenced and that the sheep had made the holes!

The company soon installed various items of plant at the quarry. There was a 90 horsepower suction gas plant and gas engine (built by Crossley Brothers) and a Blake-Marsden chipping machine capable of making 30-35 tons of chippings per day. An 18 ft-long screen was installed with an internal diameter of 2 ft 6 in. which could sort stone to a size of 2¼ inches. A 2-cylinder Tilghman air compressor was bought to drive the drills. A bunker of 240 tons capacity was constructed, also a powder magazine and huts for the sett makers. The total cost of the plant and the building of the sidings was £5,534. The first stone was sold on 1st June, 1922, though the first few years were to prove difficult ones for the company as outlets for the stone were investigated. Orders proved to be scarce and up to November 1922 the total loss on quarry operations was £106.

There was an early fatality in the quarry (in December 1922) when an engineman working the stonebreaker met his death. This resulted in the stonebreaker becoming more securely fenced.

By 21st May, 1923 just two or three men were said to be working in the quarry, though this proved to be a low point and orders picked up, so that by the end of November of the same year 43 men were at work and the profit for the year was £176. The quarry thus became a major employer in an area where alternative work was difficult to find at the time. In the same year it was realised that more customers were requesting their roadstone to be supplied in tarred form. Hence a tarring plant was purchased from Messrs F. Parker of the Viaduct Works in Leicester. The order situation continued to improve and the following became customers of the quarry: Castle Ward RDC, the Ashington Coal Co., Alnwick RDC, Morpeth RDC and Northumberland County Council.

However, two further problems arose. Firstly a local stock farmer, appropriately named Mr Herdman, complained about the layers of dust that were being deposited on his fields as a result of the stone-breaker being inadequately covered. Several of his animals were sick and some had developed tumours. The examining veterinary surgeon, Clement Elphick, MRCVS, had conducted post-mortems on the animals, and whilst he could not ascribe the cancers to the dust, he considered that the large quantity of dust in the animals' rumens was severely deleterious to their digestive systems and was affecting their health. Accordingly improved covers were extended over both the stonebreakers and the railway loading bay. The second problem arose when the quarrying activities caused a rupture of the water pipe, extending from the nearby reservoir to Howick Hall. The water supply was interrupted until the pipe was repaired. Fortunately there were large capacity tanks in the roof of the Hall where there was a few days' water supply stored.

By 1925 the quarry was still tendering for the supply of roadstone to Northumberland County Council at their depots, some located at rail stations. In 1928, for example, Howick stone was used by the council for the improvement of the Rothbury to Alnwick road, in this example the stone was being taken from the quarry by the Central Motor Transport Company's road vehicles. To illustrate the upturn in business about 13,000 tons of crushed stone left the site in 1928, together with 780 tons of setts. (The quarry was still supplying stone to Northumberland County Council into the 1930s even though they had opened some extensive quarries of their own by this time.)

The increase in stone traffic also necessitated the extension of the railway sidings to increase capacity and this was duly carried out in 1927. The quarry had been linked to the LNER East Coast main line by means of a trailing connection from the up line. This led to a pair of sidings and a loading dock adjacent to the main quarry equipment where crushed stone could be loaded directly into standard gauge main line wagons. Around four wagons were normally present for loading. The sidings were shunted by the loco of the pick-up goods en route from Tweedmouth to Alnmouth. (None of the quarry leasing companies ever operated locomotives of their own at the standard gauge

Lister L6229, built in 1935, was photographed at Howick Quarry on 22nd December, 1967 having been out of use, and removed from its rails, for a long time. Part of the quarry face and a line of rails form the backdrop.   *P.D. Nicholson*

A second view of the 2 ft gauge Lister at Howick Quarry taken from a different angle, on 23rd December, 1967. Having been out of use since mid-1961 the locomotive was purchased by P.D. Nicholson and removed to Surrey for preservation and restoration to working order.

P.D. Nicholson

Howick Sidings. The sidings remained connected to the main line for some time after rail traffic ceased, but the connection, latterly operated with a ground frame, was finally removed in the late 1960s.)

It was in 1927 that representatives of Messrs Trollope & Colls, a London based firm of civil engineers and contractors which had been incorporated in 1903, called at Howick. Colls had done pioneer work in reinforced concrete in World War I when the material was used in the construction of many docks, viaducts and railway bridges. Later the company became involved in the manufacture of concrete pipes for drainage, then later with the building of houses, garden cities and works buildings. Their interests extended as far abroad as the Far East.

Trollope & Colls wished to establish a works on Howick Estates land, adjacent to the quarry, for the purpose of making pipes and other articles, such as kerb stones from concrete. Use would be made of chipped whinstone from the quarry during the manufacture of these items. Trollope & Colls took over the site shortly afterwards, their production starting on 16th February, 1928. One early contract was for the supply of concrete kerb stones to the county council for use in Warkworth, Bamburgh and in Canongate, Alnwick. Paving slabs were also laid on pavements in the centre of Alnwick. Initially they planned to use sand, obtained 'free' from nearby Lowsteads beach, in their concrete but this proved to be too fine and ⅛ in. whinstone from the quarry was used instead.

In 1933 Earl Grey became a Director of the Howick Whinstone Co. The fees for the quarrying of stone were immediately reduced! The old rates, payable to the Howick Estates, were 1s. 6d. per ton for dressed stone and 9d. for 'other' stone. The new rates became 8d. and 5d. respectively, the difference being accounted for by the salary paid to Earl Grey as Director. The company continued to operate at a profit. However, at the start of the 1940s Trollope and Colls made overtures towards taking over the quarry interests. On 12th March, 1941 a draft lease was sent by the Howick Estates to Trollope & Colls and they ultimately assumed responsibility for the site. They operated out of Howick for many years though later the pipe works appears to have been taken over by a firm called Hepworth Building Products. Another source names the owner, some time after World War II, as Charlton Carse. Rail-mounted cranes are known to have operated on a dedicated craneway on the site for moving the heavy pipes and mouldings.

As the distance between the quarry faces and the crushers increased so it became necessary to improve movement of the stone between the two. A 2 ft gauge railway was established linking the faces to the crushers. The track layout varied according to the faces being worked upon but fundamentally consisted of a fan of tracks with sets of points allowing the 2 cwt capacity 'skip' wagons, built by Hudsons, to be supplied to the loaders. All loading was performed manually with men working in pairs at the end of each siding. Full wagons were taken to the crushers and fresh empties brought by means of a small 4-wheeled locomotive. Around 25 side-tipping skips were used in the quarry. Some small straight-sided tubs existed also, for the removal of spoil and dust.

The loaded skips were taken to the plant and emptied into a small hopper from which an elevator led up to the stone crushers. The crushed stone then

This photograph shows the original plant building at Howick Quarry. The standard gauge siding terminated here where crushed stone was loaded into wagons for movement away via the local 'pick-up goods'. The quarry's Lister was stabled beneath an awning, now disappeared, on the opposite side of this building.   *Author*

Quarry workmen from the 1920s would hardly recognise the immense Howick Quarry of the 21st century! In the background are the elevators, crushers and hoppers, whilst in the foreground is the tarmac plant. All products are now transported by road.   *Author*

Until the 1960s Howick Quarry and the pipeworks were served by a trailing connection from the East Coast up main line, controlled by Littlehoughton Ground Frame. This is the site of the former frame together with the 'gate' through which the private siding entered the works.
Author

This is a 2011 panoramic view of the Littlehoughton Pipeworks of F.P. McCann Ltd, located adjacent to the Howick Quarry. This works formerly had a craneway with two cranes for moving their pipes and mouldings around the works yard. Originally some of the works products left by rail but now all are removed by road. *Author*

One of the cranes is in action on the craneway at Howick pipe works. The works was established by Trollope & Colls in the 1920s and passed through several ownerships, before becoming part of F.P. McCann Ltd. *F.P. McCann Ltd*

After removal from Howick to a site in Surrey, Lister 6299 was quickly restored to working condition. On 28th August, 1971 it is seen at Farnham Town Show, on a temporarily laid track, giving rides to the general public. It is now to be found at the Devon Railway Centre, near Tiverton. *P.D. Nicholson*

passed over the screens and fell into hoppers awaiting transfer to the main line rail wagons or into road lorries. At night and during works holidays, also at the time of stone blasting, the locomotive was stabled adjacent to the plant where there was an overhanging awning. Any necessary maintenance and fuelling was carried out here.

Only one locomotive is known to have been used at Howick. This was a four-wheel petrol-engined machine, with mechanical transmission, built by Lister & Co. (Works No. L6299/1935). It was built in 1935. It arrived 'second-hand', having been purchased by Trollope & Colls, from John Board & Co. of Dunball, near Bridgwater, in Somerset. Board's operated a Portland Cement and Limeworks at the Dunball site where they operated, at different times, several steam, petrol- and diesel-engined locomotives on a tramway linking their quarry and works. Board's had originally bought the engine new from Lister's. (Its rail system closed and track was lifted in 1954.) When No. 6299 arrived at Howick it bore no name or operating number. It was used to move loaded tippers towards the conveyor and crushers, to return empties to the sidings at the quarry faces and to move the wagons of spoil to a tip. As it was the only locomotive at Howick, on the occasions when it was briefly out of action, it was necessary for the quarry workmen to propel their wagons by hand.

Eventually, by about 1961, the rail system was taken out of use, as large excavators replaced much of the labour force. The locomotive, fortunately, was not scrapped but was purchased and restored to working order by Mr P.D. Nicholson and kept at the Brockham Museum Trust at Dorking in Surrey. Later it was moved to the Devon Railway Centre at Bickleigh Mill, Cadleigh station, near Tiverton in Devon, where it survives 'in preservation'. Some of the tubs and skips survived in the quarry until 1968 but were then disposed of.

Today the quarry at Howick is leased by the TARMAC group and all of the stone is removed by road, various hauliers being used. The original plant has long since been replaced by very much larger, more efficient, equipment. The site of the original plant survives by the side of the present-day visitors' car park. The main line and narrow gauge rails have long-since been removed, though a gate survives in the fence close to the main line.

As mentioned earlier, a pipe-construction factory was built adjacent to the quarry. This was constructed during World War II and produced pipes for drainage and sewerage. Before its construction a 'reservoir' supplying Howick Hall was located on the site, lying along an approximate east-west axis. Early Works Managers included a Mr Pickup and later a Mr Foot, but later the Manager was a local man, Ian Shiel. The Ordnance Survey maps of the 1970s show the extent of the craneway but it has now been removed and all evidence has disappeared. The craneway had two cranes, a smaller one of 2-ton capacity and 'the big crane' whose driver was Bob Armstrong, a local man from Howick. Another who drove the cranes for a time was Ken Venus. Fortunately a photograph survives of one of the cranes on the craneway, though unfortunately the top part of its jib is out-of-picture.

The pipeworks is now the Alnwick Plant of F.P. McCann Ltd, of Knockloughrim, Magherafelt, County Londonderry. They are specialist manufacturers of concrete pipes, manholes, inspection chambers, fittings and ancillary products and a huge store of these products, covering several hectares, is found on site.

Both of these large industrial complexes are located at the end of a long signposted drive from the Littlehoughton Road. This drive is private property and narrow in places and is used frequently by large articulated lorries arriving and leaving the two works.

16 - *The Longhoughton and Ratcheugh Quarry Railways*

Longhoughton and Ratcheugh Quarries (NU235156 and NU230152 respectively), are located to the north of the unclassified road leading from what is now the B1340 road at Denwick, to the villages of Longhoughton and Boulmer. They lie on the side of Howlet Hill about three miles east-north-east of Alnwick.

Longhoughton Quarry runs in an approximately north-easterly direction from its entrance gate onto the Denwick-Longhoughton road. Longhoughton Quarry has been quarried for both limestone and whinstone, though the latter was of greater importance. Recently Longhoughton Quarry has become a site of some international geological importance. At Longhoughton igneous whinstone was forced to the surface next to rocks of the Great Limestone series. The heat and pressure caused some of the limestone to become 'contact-metamorphosed' into a type of marble. Some recent research has been conducted into this by scientists from Green University, and it receives regular visits from other learned groups.

Next to it, and running in an approximately westerly direction from the same gate, lies Ratcheugh Quarry. Ratcheugh has always been purely a whinstone quarry and is still being worked intermittently. The last operators erected a small bank around the site and planted small trees and shrubs to landscape the surroundings and make the quarry less visible from the public road.

A very small quarry, at the point where Ratcheugh and Longhoughton meet, is recorded on the first Ordnance Survey maps. This quarry must have been developed after about 1830 because there is no trace of the quarry on maps and plans dating from this time. By the publication date of the OS maps of the 1890s, a small extension had been made to Ratcheugh Quarry whilst Longhoughton Quarry had been considerably extended. By the early 1920s there had been little further development at Ratcheugh but Longhoughton had been extended both north-eastwards and eastwards, with stone being removed from two levels. One new development at this time was the appearance on the map of a new, quite extensive, quarry to the east of the main Longhoughton Quarry. This had its own gate exit onto the Denwick-Longhoughton road. It was simply marked 'Quarry' on maps, with no other name specified. The area around the quarries was not re-surveyed until the mid-1950s. By this time Ratcheugh Quarry was being extended westwards and Longhoughton Quarry was similarly increasing in size with northwards and eastwards extensions resulting in the complete disappearance of one field. It is on maps of this period that the quarry tramway is first shown, serving both Ratcheugh and Longhoughton. The 'new' quarry, to the east, appears not to have been much used for it is shown on maps as covering approximately the same area as 30 years previously. This quarry may have been filled in during the 1970s or early 1980s for it is not shown on later maps. Meanwhile Ratcheugh had almost quadrupled in size by the 1980s and Longhoughton had been extended northwards, with several quarry faces being worked. For the first time the quarry was identified as 'Longhoughton Quarry (Whinstone)'. Ratcheugh Quarry, surprisingly, had never been separately named on maps. The 1980s maps were the first to show the quarries with the railways removed and stone conveyors installed. The latest maps correctly mark Longhoughton Quarry as 'disused'; once again Ratcheugh Quarry, though still intermittently worked, is not separately identified!

The failure to name Ratcheugh Quarry, and the small later quarry, on maps and in documents, has led to some some difficulty and confusion as to the operators of each quarry. Furthermore all of the quarries have actually been *leased* from the Northumberland Estates though various printed material refers to the 'quarry owners'!

Two main concerns have been involved with quarrying in the locality. The first on the scene was the Northumberland Whinstone Co. Ltd. This concern was incorporated on 8th November, 1876. It operated other quarries elsewhere in Northumberland, notably at Barrasford (from 1876 to the end of the 1950s) and at Greenhead, near Hadrian's Wall (between 1885 and 1952). This firm was known to be working at Longhoughton in 1887 when John Lamb was the quarry manager. At this time the quarry was paying a rent of 6*d*. per ton for setts and kerbs with 2*d*. per ton being paid for rough stone and rubble. By 1902 there had been a change of manager at Longhoughton, Andrew Anderson having assumed the position, but he had been replaced by a Mr Coxon by 1911. In 1922 it is recorded that just two workers were employed in the quarrying of limestone at Longhoughton but 49 were involved in the removal of whinstone at Ratcheugh. It is not known whether this figure referred to the total of whinstone quarrymen at both quarries. This is likely, for whinstone, in addition to limestone, was being removed from Longhoughton at this time. By 1925 a trade directory incorrectly identified the company as 'owners' but recorded David Turnbull as quarry manager. It was the Northumberland Whinstone Quarry which introduced the tramway system in the quarry and later replaced it with a system of conveyors to take the stone to the crushers and screens. The crushed stone was always taken from the quarries by road vehicles. In earlier years this would have been by carts pulled by horses, later motorized vehicles were used. Some was delivered directly to local destinations whilst other stone was taken to the nearby Longhoughton sidings where it was loaded into wagons for onward movement by rail. As an illustration of how busy this station yard could be, the North Eastern Railway's records of 1913 indicate that 26,249 tons of roadstone and 3,875 tons of building stone were loaded there onto railway wagons.

The second concern to have operated at Longhoughton was H.G. Prowde Ltd, though they are often referred to at Longhoughton and elsewhere as 'McLaren and Prowde' or even as 'McLaren and Prowde Ltd', though there was never a registered company of that name. H.G. Prowde Ltd was officially

This photograph was taken on 14th July, 1968 and shows a pair of Hudson Hunslet locomotives several years after being taken out of service at Longhoughton Quarry. Nearest the camera is HE1992 built in 1939 and furthest away is HE1947 built in 1938. Both were scrapped in September 1969. *P.D. Nicholson*

It has not been possible for the author to discover any photographs of locomotives at work at Longhoughton. However, HE1942 was photographed working at Barrasford Quarry before the Northumberland Whinstone Company transferred it to Longhoughton some time after July 1959. *Jim Peden/Industrial Railway Society*

incorporated 'around 1917' according to Companies House. In practice they had already been operating for at least 20 years! In 1896 'H.G. Prowde Ltd', then unregistered, obtained a lease enabling a start to be made on quarrying at Longhoughton. The Directors of the company were Henry Gordon Prowde (of 22 St Bede's Terrace, Sunderland), Dr E.C. Prowde, E. Prowde (described as a married woman), J. Wilton, a widow, all of the same Sunderland address, also William Edwards, a civil engineer of Wylam, and George McLaren of 'Woodhead', Christon Bank. The lease was for the quarrying of both limestone and whinstone. Prowde obtained a further lease in 1919. Consideration of these dates and the evidence on the Ordnance Survey maps leads to the conclusion that Prowde was the operator of the 'new' quarry that first appeared on the 1920s maps and which failed to show significant subsequent development. There is no evidence that Prowde ever operated a tramway or railway within his quarry despite the 'standard' terms of the lease which would have permitted him to do so.

Evidence as regards the working of the tramway within the Longhoughton and Ratcheugh quarries is derived both from map evidence and the oral evidence of two quarrymen, one of whom recalls the operation of the line in the early 1940s and one who started to work at the quarry in the 1950s. The lines extended into both quarries and there were several moveable sidings leading to the faces where stone was being obtained. The lines led over the weighbridge and to the winch where loaded wagons were raised up to the level of the crushers which were in an elevated position at the top of the quarry face near its entrance. Both quarrymen recall only 'two or so', locomotives working at any one time. However a total of seven locomotives is recorded as operating at the site at different times. The first two were ex-War Department Light Railway (WDLR) Motorail 4-wheel petrol-engined machines with mechanical transmission. Their works numbers were MR1346/1918 and 1381/1918; their WDLR numbers were 3067 and 3102 respectively but they did not carry fleet numbers whilst at Longhoughton. Later arrivals were all built by the Hunslet Engine Co. and were 4-wheel diesel-mechanical machines. HE2848/1943 arrived new from the manufacturers whilst HE1885/1938 arrived from the company's Greenhead Quarry by July 1952, as did HE1952/1941. The final two locomotives came from the company's Barrasford Quarry. These were HE1947/1938 (arrived by April 1958) and 1992/1939 (arriving after July 1959). No. 1346 was later sold or scrapped, 1381 went to Robert Brett & Sons in Kent by 1950. Nos. 2848, 1885 and 1952 were all sold or scrapped leaving just Nos. 1947 and 1992 on site at the time of the cessation of locomotive working in about 1963-64. These last two locomotives were scrapped in September 1969. Fortunately they were photographed on-site in July 1968, though by this time they were becoming derelict. No. 1947 was bearing 'No. 1' on the back of its cab at this time.

Industrial Railway Society records suggest that there may have been another locomotive used at Longhoughton, namely a four-wheeled vertical-boilered Sentinel (actually S6770 but carrying the maker's plates of 6751). This might have come to the quarry in the late 1920s. It had, according to some records, moved to Barrasford Quarry by July 1947. However, one quarry employee who worked at Longhoughton in the 1940s has no recollections of this locomotive. It

Above: Longhoughton Quarry in 2011 is largely filled with a lake which provides private fishing for a local angling club. A footpath linking the Alnwick Road and Longhoughton village runs adjacent to the lake and is frequented by dog walkers and ramblers.

Author

Right: The concrete remains of the bases of the Longhoughton Quarry crushers remain at the end of the stone face on its south side, to the right of the track leading into the quarry. Encroaching vegetation is making their photography more and more difficult. Part of the quarry has been partially landscaped and new trees and shrubs have been planted.

Author

may have worked at Northumberland Whinstone's other quarry at Greenhead.

The role of the locomotives was, as might be expected: to deliver empty wagons to the quarrymen at the working faces and remove the full wagons to the winch which hauled the wagons as far as the weighbridge, and then up a steep slope, for the stone to be tipped into the crushers. There was no shed for housing the locomotives at night or when under repair. At the end of the shift at least one of the diesels would be driven part-way up the slope (near the winch) and then braked. In the morning the downslope would be used to 'bump-start' the diesel engine when the brake was released. In the 1950s there were just over 20 small side-tippers in use in the quarry, referred to as 'the tubs'. One quarryman recalls that all the quarrymen loading the tubs were 'pieceworkers' and worked singly. They were paid according to how much stone they could load into the tubs each day. The tubs had small tokens attached, corresponding to each quarryman, before they were weighed. The tokens were returned to the quarryman, with the empty tub, after weighing and tipping. Between 1926 and 1929 at least, the quarry possessed a tarmacadam plant and tendered for the supply of tarred stone to Northumberland County Council. Later, by 1953, some of the men at the quarry were also engaged in making setts, kerb stones and similar dressed stones. These were cut from larger stones which had not been 'burned' by the explosives when the rock was blasted. Later kerb stones were made from concrete. In the days of the railway the quarry was producing about 300 tons of stone per day. Later, when large dumper trucks and conveyors came into use, the quarry was much more productive, producing over 1,000 tons per day with reduced manpower. A single blast could free 4,000 tons of rock from the whinstone face when large stones were not required. One shift per day was worked at the quarry: workers started at 7.30 am, stopped for a 15 minute tea-break at 9.00 am, ate their 'dinner' between noon and 12.30 pm and finished work at 4.15 pm. Longhoughton Quarry finally closed in 1974, though Ratcheugh has continued to be worked intermittently.

Today, Longhoughton Quarry is a designated site of special scientific interest on account of its special whin sill exposures. It can be visited via a signposted footpath connecting the Denwick-Longhoughton Road and Longhoughton village. Part of the quarry is now flooded and the small lake is used for angling. The remainder of the quarry forms a small park which is a haven for wild life. The adjacent Ratcheugh Quarry has ceased to be a working quarry though piles of crushed stone abound. Some potential tenants are showing an interest. Large vehicles formerly entered and left the site. It was last operated by Bardon Aggregates, part of Aggregate Industries, themselves part of the HOLCIM Group of Companies. Bardon Aggregates are specialist suppliers of crushed rock, gravel, sand and aggregate, including rail ballast, sea defence materials and surface dressings to the construction industry. The filled-in site of the former 'new' quarry operated by H.G. Prowde's company is now occupied by a local builder, Gary Mallaburn.

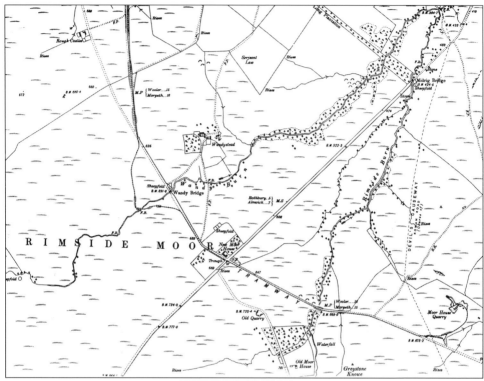

Above: The southernmost section of the he Moor House quarry railway appeared on an Ordnance Survey map in the 1920s. However, for some reason, the more northern section extending on towards the Bridge of Aln and Whittingham station did not appear on the adjacent map sheet.

Right: The remains of the base of the elevator and crusher survive near to the quarry close to the A697 Morpeth to Wooler road. The former trackbed leading from the quarry can be seen following the ledge on line on the hillside above these remains.

Author

Chapter Six

The Quarry Railways of Northumberland County Council

Northumberland County Council has, for many years, required sources of roadstone both for the making of tarmacadam and as a top dressing for its roads. The stone has been supplied both by privately-owned quarries and the council's own quarries. Some of the county council quarry sites are in the south and west of the county and are beyond the scope of this book. However there were three major sources of stone, owned or leased by the county council, within the Berwick and Alnwick Districts, namely the quarries at Moor House and Hare Crag situated not far from Alnwick, and the terrace of the River Breamish. This river terrace lies to the west of the Morpeth to Wooler main road (now the A697), near to the former Hedgeley station and Powburn village. One other 'planned' county council railway, at Middleton Hall, is referred to in Chapter Nine.

17 – The Moor House Railway

A Northumberland County Council quarry railway system, of two foot gauge, was formerly located adjacent to the A697, Morpeth to Wooler 'turnpike' road, close to where it forms a crossroads with the B6341 linking Alnwick with Rothbury. A small quarry at Moor House had existed before its use by the County Council but had been closed for many years.

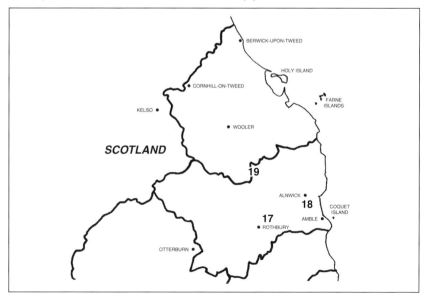

The line of railway opened soon after the end of World War I. It linked the whinstone quarry at Moor House (NU113059) with a more northerly section of the A697 road which had been proposed for upgrading. This work involved the widening of the carriageway, construction of new embankments and the excavation of some shallow cuttings. The Minutes of the Roads & Bridges Committee refer to the improvements being made at locations from Weldon Bridge, near Longframlington, as far as Whittingham station. At the same time stone was required to resurface the road from Roughley Wood to the main road, which was almost impassable as a result of the damage caused by the movement of heavy timber wagons in the vicinity. The committee Chairman did not propose to enter into a formal lease with the landowner, Sir Hubert Swinburne of Capheaton. Instead he had been in touch with the Capheaton land agent and it was agreed that the necessary machinery could be moved to the Moor House Quarry site. This included a stone breaker, screen, engine and loading dock, plus a hut for the men to live in at the quarry. The estimated cost of the initial work was £1,000 and it was considered, by the committee, that no more than 6d. per ton should be paid for the stone. Swinburne's agent agreed to this. In practice the estimated sum of £1,000 was slightly exceeded! Initially the railway, ultimately just over 4½ miles in length, was laid on the verge alongside the main road and there was no need for wayleave payments over Sir Hubert's land.

In September 1920 plant arrived on site, the first recorded in the council's Roads & Bridges Committee Minutes being seven double-sided tippers (costing £24 10s. 0d. each) and eight end-tippers (costing £26 14s. 0d. each). The same supplier, Ord & Maddison, provided a stone breaker for £214 10s. 0d. A steam engine, to power the stone breaker, was provided for £200. A revolving screen was ordered from, and supplied, by Ords for the sum of £325. A vertical lift was also ordered to aid the removal of overburden (£250). This was driven by a petrol engine.

In February 1921 the Motor Rail & Tramcar Co. accepted a tender for two 20 horse power petrol locomotives of 24 in. gauge. One, numbered MR2115 of 1921, a four-wheeled petrol-mechanical locomotive, was delivered to Whittingham station by the NER. It was then taken to Moor House by road and initially kept in the open air. (A locomotive shed was not erected until the second half of 1923.) The other was probably delivered to another county council site. September 1921 saw the arrival of new sleepers and rails as the line was extended. Hudson's supplied 10 sets of points and crossings, also four turntables (three of which were located at the quarry). They also supplied 12 extra side-tippers, which were described as 'strong and most suitable'. Some 'wood bogies' were supplied, in 1922, by the firm of Wooley & Willis who also supplied some new pointwork. Sleepers, 300 in number, were obtained from R.F. & F.W. Brown. At this time some 20 men were employed at the quarry and on the railway. By November 1921 the quarry was reported as 'working' but there was an immediate need for 12 more 'bogies'. Six more ½ ton tippers arrived in 1922.

It had been reported in the Roads & Bridges Committee Minutes that Moorhouse Quarry [sic] required two 'motor tractor' locomotives. However, only one appeared in the inventory of 3rd September, 1923 when there was a reference to just '1 haulage engine'. (The inventory also listed the following other items: a timber with felt roof men's cabin, a tractor shed, an office, a blacksmith's shop, an iron engine shed, a petrol store, a 10 hp engine, one crusher, two tractors, several trucks, one petrol pump, one water tank and one tarmacadam mixer.) The reference to just one locomotive is puzzling. Industrial Railway Society (IRS) records show that a former War Department Light Railway locomotive (No. LR2946), a 4-wheeled petrol-engined locomotive with mechanical transmission number MR1225, had been at Moor House since the first half of 1920 (IRS records say 'before 23rd July, 1920'), at which time enquiries about spares had been made! Also No. MR2115 had been delivered in 1921. Perhaps one of the locomotives was away 'on loan' or for repairs when the inventory was drawn up.

In August 1925, W.H. Baxter's supplied new jaw stock and toggle bearings for the stone crusher and Motor Rail supplied axles and wheels (two pairs), possibly for Moor House, possibly for Powburn.

Railway lines with wagon turntables served the various quarry faces. From the quarry loaded wagons were hauled round a curve up a steep gradient leading towards the main (now A697) road, adjacent to which was the 'works' with its crushers, screens and a loading hopper. An elevator fed stone to the crushers. Crushed gravel was then emptied into tipper wagons that were hauled by one of the small locomotives up a continuation of the gradient towards the main road, which was then crossed on the level. Gates protected the road crossing. The rails then followed the line of the road on a verge on its western side, crossing the Rimside Burn on a bridge. The line then descended as it approached the Moor House crossroads. Here there appears to have been another set of gates, normally open to road traffic, which prevented the trains crossing over the Alnwick-Rothbury road without a stop. Originally, beyond the level crossing at the crossroads, the line hugged the roadside as it headed towards Whittingham. However, this straight alignment necessitated steep gradients and the locomotives struggled to cope. A westwards deviation was made, over the land of Sir Hubert, before a bridge took the line over the Wandy Burn. This burn was some 40 ft below the level of Moor House crossroads. The rail bridge was a timber trestle which was located a few yards downstream from a lower-level pedestrian footbridge across the same burn. The bridge carried the line of rails several feet above the burn which drains the water from Rimside Moor. Beyond the bridge the line continued on an embankment curving in a more northerly direction back towards the A697 road and meeting its original alignment close to the junction of the main road with the then largely unfenced track, now a metalled road, leading towards Thrunton Wood. This new line proved successful and the locomotives could cope with the more gentle gradients of the deviation.

At the Thrunton Wood Road junction there was another level crossing and the line crossed over to the eastern side of the Wooler road which it followed it for about another 600 metres, according to the 1921-surveyed OS map. However, in subsequent years embankments and cuttings were built for the road to the north of this point and the line was eventually extended towards Whittingham station.

A gorse bush grows on the former trackbed leading up from Moor House Quarry on the right of this picture whilst in the foreground several tracks formerly led towards the location of the elevator and crusher, the remains of which project above the long grass.   *Author*

This view, looking from the Whittingham direction and taken next to the A697 road, looks back towards Moor House. The former rail alignment crosses from left to right in the foreground. It then descends, directly away from the photographer, using the embankment leading towards the site of the former bridge over the Wandy Burn. When first built the line followed the main road more closely employing steeper gradients.   *Author*

The 1921 map showed no passing loops on the 'main line' of the railway. It may be that the trains of loaded wagons were hauled by the locomotive from the crushers to the site of use, with 'empties' being propelled back. However, it is likely that as the line was extended towards Whittingham station in the mid-1920s that loops were provided, especially if two locomotives were in use at one time. A small passing loop certainly existed at the site of the 'works'. This allowed a locomotive to run-round the wagons which it had hauled from the quarry so as to propel them towards the crushers; the running-round process would be repeated so that 'empties' could be propelled back down to the quarry, thus ensuring that the locomotive was not 'trapped'.

The closure of the Moor House Quarry on 31st December, 1928 was recorded in the Roads & Bridges Committee Minutes, following the completion of the road improvements. No mention is made of any sale of plant, some of which may have been transferred away to other county council quarries. It is known that one of the locomotives was transferred to Breamish Gravel Depot, Powburn, towards the end of the 1920s. It performed useful work at Powburn after which it was eventually sold or scrapped. The disposal of the Moor House wagons seems not to have been recorded though they may have accompanied the locomotive for further use at Powburn or been transferred elsewhere.

What remains of the line today? Moor House Quarry is located on private land and permission must be sought to visit it. The faces of the whinstone can be seen in the main quarry though its centre has now filled up with water forming a small pond complete with resident waterfowl. Stone extraction from the northwards extension of the quarry, shown on the 1921 map, clearly ceased quite early in the quarry's life as little stone was removed from here and its level is some metres above the rest of the quarry. The exit from the quarry is now very marshy in the winter months. The tips of dumped quarry spoil are now covered with largely impenetrable gorse bushes. The curved gradient up to the 'works' can be followed as it is grassy and slightly better drained than some of the surrounding moorland. The track layout in the works area can be made out in part, though the Millstone Burn, which now flows through the site, makes 'detective work' difficult, especially after rain! Some remains of the base of the crushing plant or screens are visible from the fence at the side of the main road. The wide verge on the western side of the A697 indicates the route of the line to the Moor House crossroads and the trackbed can be followed quite easily to beyond the Wandy Burn. As at the 'works' site, the partly-grassy trackbed is better drained than the surrounding marshy moorland with its sedges and bracken. Apart from the rather precipitous edge to the valley sides adjacent to the Wandy Burn, there is no evidence of bridge remains (either of the railway- or the foot-bridge) though close to the Thrunton road junction the grass-covered embankment stands out very clearly. Once again this section is on private land. To the north of this junction there are no visible remains of the line.

This panoramic view shows the quarry face at Hare Crag with numerous tippers awaiting loading by hand with stone which has been dislodged from the quarry faces by blasting. It is fortunate that photographers such as Chris Down and Peter Nicholson visited the quarry to record these details before the quarry closed.   *Dr C.G. Down*

Another of Chris Down's photographs shows a huge fan of tracks extending right up to the quarry faces. One of the quarry locomotives is seen assembling a train of loaded wagons to be taken along the main line to the plant next to the A1 road by one of the more powerful locomotives.   *Dr C.G. Down*

18 - The Hare Crag Railway

The Minutes of the Northumberland County Council Roads & Bridges Committee, dated 4th April, 1921, indicate that improvements needed to be carried out to the Felton to Alnwick section of the 'Great North Road', now the A1. It was considered that the old Hare Crag Quarry, located to the west of the road (NU153075) and west of Shilbottle village, could be reopened and would be very suitable for providing the 16,000 tons of stone necessary for the improvements. The quarry landlord, the Duke of Northumberland, agreed to allow stone to be removed for 6d. per ton with an annual rent of £10 per annum.

The council moved quickly for by 25th July, 1921 the first 'Simplex' locomotive had been delivered for the railway at the quarry (at a cost of £641 15s. 0d.). This was MR2118/21 and it arrived via Alnwick station. Already on 4th July, Hudson's had delivered some tipper wagons and some points, crossings and sleepers, and some rails arrived on the following day. By December 1921 the quarry was reported to need 12 extra 'bogies'. By the start of 1922 Ingersolls had supplied a jackhammer to the quarry. Further rolling stock arrived, 12 elegant Hudson side-tippers, with elaborately made trunnions, being delivered via Alnwick station and 'wood bogies' were supplied by Wooley & Willis. By 1923 the committee had been told of the introduction of a tar mixing plant at Hare Crag. By September 1923 it was reported that the operations there greatly exceeded those at Moor House. An inventory, dated 3rd September, gives some idea of the scale of operations. It shows that since the quarry had been reopened, just two years previously, two living huts had been constructed for the men. Also there was a loading gantry, a petrol store, office, tractor house, weigh house, tool store, engine house, blacksmith's shop and a gantry for the tramway. The tar plant had a boiler, tar tank, three tar boilers and a tarmac mixer. There was a weighbridge, two tractors, a portable forge, a portable engine, an air compressor, a portable stone breaker or crusher, and a fuel tank generator. Soon after this it was necessary to obtain some spare parts for the stone breaker.

The distance from the then-current quarry face to the works at the main road (NU174081) was about 1.4 miles but the total amount of trackwork, including all sidings, later amounted to almost two miles. The main quarry face had been supplemented by a further extension to the south. Trains on the tramway were reported to be moving six tons of stone per journey in the early days. Much of the stone from the quarry was converted into macadam though some was transported away for use as a road top-dressing. A local firm, T. Muckle & Son, had successfully tendered for this.

A new 21-year lease, dated 23rd March, 1931 was negotiated with the Duke. Various conditions were attached, such the need to erect wire fencing alongside the tramway and at the A1 roadside site. In addition the lessees would have to maintain all necessary gates with compensation to be paid to the owners of nearby Snipe Farm of £25 for the nuisance caused by the tramway. The tramway wayleave proposed was £40 per annum, the ground rent as £12 per annum with 6d. per ton royalties being paid on the first 10,000 tons extracted each year. Once negotiations were complete the parties agreed on a 'certain rent' of £150 for the first 6,000 tons, all other figures being the same.

On the 15th July, 1968, shortly before the closure of the system, Hunslet locomotive HE2834 (No. 6 in the Hare Crag numbering system) shunts three tipper wagons towards the quarry face. This locomotive was formerly employed at Powburn in the Breamish Valley until the works there closed.   *P.D. Nicholson*

In this view two trains with loaded wagons of stone from the quarry follow successively along the undulating main line towards the plant at the eastern end of the line.   *Dr C.G. Down*

The county council continued to invest in the quarry: new blasting equipment arrived, a new corrugated roof and skylights were fitted to the 'traction shed' and the tramway trackwork was upgraded with the laying of 500 new sleepers. New buildings were constructed in the quarry, the Choppington Brick Co. supplying 20,000 bricks for these. By 1932 mullions and drainpipes had arrived for these buildings, new steel channel arrived for the quarry weighbridge, new conveyor belting arrived and electric heaters were installed for the new plant. Alongside this a new control panel was installed for regulating the 440 volt electrical supply to the plant including the elevators, screens and crushers. By this time, of the 44 men employed at the quarry, 29 lived in Alnwick with wife or family, whilst others lived at, for example, Newton-on-the-Moor, Felton, Longhorsley or Shilbottle. Some men over-nighted in a bothy at Hare Crag on weekday nights but went home at weekends.

After the completion of the A1 upgrade, demand for Hare Crag stone remained at a high level. It became used in various parts of the county. By 1948 the total of stone extracted had reached 150 tons per day, some 50,000 tons in the year, the stone being used mainly for roadstone but also for concrete aggregate. At this time the quarry contained two shelters, a pump house, an office, blacksmith's shop, also a canteen and store. Some of the quarry faces were up to 50 ft in height. All blasting at the quarry took place in the morning, with the rest of the day being taken up with loading the stone into tubs. This loading was never mechanized; all was done by hand. By the main road there was an office, loading gantries, the loco shed, crushing plant, screens, conveyors and the tarmacadam plant. In 1950 the quarry was further enlarged, though some of the old parts of the quarry were starting to be filled in. Eventually, in 1969 the County Council closed the quarry, though in the 1970s it was briefly handed over to Alan Davison Construction of Houghton-le-Spring. This concern removed about 100,000 tons of stone from 2 hectares, using road vehicles. Eventually, in 1976, the fate of the quarry was sealed. The decision was taken to start filling in the quarry with domestic rubbish and other landfill material. Tipping started in 1980 with two million tons of rubbish being dumped at the site over a period of just over 20 years.

Plans exist, bearing several different dates, which illustrate the extent of the 2 ft gauge tramway or railway system at Hare Crag. The 'main line', laid with sections of prefabricated rail, linked the quarries with the tarmacadam plant and loading gantries by the main road. Many lines served the individual quarry faces. At any one time there could be a dozen such sidings in use with an equal number not being used. Other sidings existed to hold the 'empties' before they were moved to the faces. Various loops led to the main line which exited the quarry and headed eastwards towards the Great North Road. Passing loops were originally located approximately one-third and two-thirds of the way between the quarry exit and the roadside plant. These loops were removed by 1948 and a modified system of working the trains was introduced. Locomotives were stabled overnight at the loco shed at the main road end of the line. Minor repairs to the locomotives were carried out here. A 'paddy train', consisting of three metal-roofed four-wheeled wagons with canvas sides was kept in a siding here overnight, ready to take men up to the quarry at the start of their shift.

The quarry plant next to the A1 road, at the eastern end of the railway, included loading gantries, a tarmacadam plant, conveyors, a crushing plant and screens. These two views were taken at this end of the line and several of these features are visible. The small tubs in the upper picture are well charged with hand-loaded rocks of regular size.   *(Both) Dr C.G. Down*

Locomotives No. 2 (HE2284) and No. 4 (HE2938) are pictured attached to a train of empty wagons within Hare Crag Quarry whilst No. 1 (HE2286) is attached to a full train before the load is taken along the main line to the eastern end of the line. No. 6 (HE2834), in the far background, appears to be the quarry pilot responsible for marshalling the wagons at the quarry faces.

Dr C.G. Down

The Hare Crag quarry and rail system, especially the 'main line', can be rather exposed in inclement weather. The driver of locomotive No. 4 (HE2938), on the right of the picture, must rely on a tarpaulin slung over the cab for some protection whilst locomotive No. 2 (HE2284) appears to be fitted with some weatherboarding on one cabside. *Dr C.G. Down*

Carrying its Hare Crag fleet number 2, Hunslet diesel-mechanical HE2284 hauls a train of six wagons along the main line. The locomotive crews appreciated the cab side sheets giving protection from the weather as this is a rather exposed location.   *Dr C.G. Down*

The driver of this train has successfully brought his train from the quarry to the plant and slowly hauls the six wagons over the wagon weighbridge so that their individual weights can be recorded. The locomotives shown are No. 1 (*left*) and No. 2.   *Dr C.G. Down*

During the day the 'paddy train' was stabled in a spare siding at the entrance to the quarry before transporting the men back to the main road at the end of the day. At the roadside end of the line there were sidings for the 'fulls' awaiting processing and also for the 'empties' awaiting transfer back to the quarry. Other sidings served the repair shop and the tarmac plant. The tipping dock ('gantry') was elevated and it could prove a difficult task for the locomotives to move the wagons up the gradient, especially in wet conditions.

Originally the line was operated by several Motor Rail 'Simplex' locomotives. Later these were replaced by Hudson-Hunslet four-wheeled diesels. To the end one Simplex was employed at the site, the final one being the petrol-engined bow-framed MR1217, which had arrived from Powburn when the system there was closed in the 1960s. This locomotive had a very brief working day. It was used solely at the start of each shift to push-start the diesel engines of the Hudson-Hunslets! Its own engine was started by turning a crank. Once the diesel engines had started the Simplex's petrol engine was switched off.

The first Simplex locomotive to arrive (MR2118) was mentioned above. The two other Simplex locomotives were MR1217 which arrived at Hare Crag having had periods of work at the county council's quarry at Closehead, Otterburn, and Breamish Gravel Works at Powburn, and MR3687 which had also worked at Powburn and was, at one time, identified as 'No. 6'. Both of these were fitted with 20 hp 2-cylinder Dorman engines. A 4-wheeled petrol-mechanical locomotive built by F.C. Hibberd, Works No. FH1770/1931, arrived new to the site and six Hunslet four-wheeled diesel-mechanical locomotives are known to have worked at Hare Crag. The first two, with fleet numbers 'No. 1' and 'No. 2' were fitted with McLaren Ricardo engines of 30 hp. They hauled most of the heavy trains on the system's main line. Their works numbers were HE2286/41 and HE2284/41 respectively. The remaining four, bearing fleet numbers from 'No. 3' to 'No. 6', were a few years younger but only fitted with 20 hp 'Ailsa Craig' engines. Their works numbers were HE2838/44, HE2938/44, HE2940/44 and HE2834/44. These locomotives were generally employed in shunting in the quarry. The Hibberd and Hudson-Hunslet locomotives were fitted with cabs to give some protection to their driver. A recently-discovered document indicates that another Hunslet, 2939/1944 was delivered in 1946 along with the locomotives 2938 and 2949 mentioned above. It is possible that it was dismantled on arrival for use as a source of spares for the other locomotives.

In the early years of the quarry's operation trains of 'fulls' and trains of empties' would pass each other at the loops on the main line. In later years two trains of fulls would traverse the line, one behind the other. The more powerful Hunslets were able to haul trains of six tubs, with a total load of about 15 tons. All tubs would be taken over the weighbridge, for each one was tagged with the identity of the quarryman that had filled it. He would be paid according to the amount of stone he had loaded into his tub. The main line locomotives could haul about 10 tubs on the return journey. Often one of the locomotives would return to the quarry 'light engine' following a train of empties hauled by another. Whilst returning the empties the diesels would maintain a good speed. With a train of 'fulls' it was mainly first gear work!

A short distance to the east of Hare Crag quarry the 'main line' crosses the infant Hampeth Burn by means of an overbridge. In the upper picture a short train of just two 'empties' has just crossed this bridge in the hands of No. 2 (HE2284) whilst in the lower picture No. 1 (HE2286) hauls a longer train of empties over the bridge and onwards towards the quarry.

(Both) Dr C.G. Down

Locomotives No. 3 (HE2838) and no. 4 (HE2938) are parked at the east end of the line in front of the 'paddy train'. The driver of No.3 must use a length of tarpaulin to keep out the weather. Many of the other locomotives were fitted with metal doors. *Dr C.G. Down*

It is very pleasing that Chris Down's photographic coverage of Hare Crag was so comprehensive. Here the three vehicles of the 'paddy train' are parked in a siding. This train transported quarry workers to and from the quarry at the start and end of shifts. The vehicles were fitted with seats and side sheets to offer protection against the weather, but offered no other luxuries! *Dr C.G. Down*

This view looks westwards along the main line towards the quarry which is located over a mile away. The line entering from the left led from the locoshed and sidings whilst the line to the right was the main wagon line towards the unloading point. The gate prevented sheep from entering into the works area.   *Dr C.G. Down*

Hare Crag was an extensive quarry with several quarry faces. Lines within the quarry were often lifted and moved from worked-out areas to the faces currently being quarried for stone. Here we see the route of a disused branch line leading from some closed quarry faces which can be seen in the background.   *Dr C.G. Down*

Each day two of the smaller locomotives generally worked in the quarry. They had several jobs. Firstly they had to ensure that the quarrymen at their workplaces had a supply of tubs for loading good stone. Occasionally it would be necessary to move other tubs to a workplace if a minor fall deposited rubble which needed removal. Full tubs had to be moved from each of the workplaces and then assembled into trains ready for the main line engines. From time to time it was necessary to shunt wagons, carrying short lengths of track to new loading points. Each locomotive driver had a mate whose responsibility was the coupling and uncoupling of wagons, changing of points and 'chocking' the wheels of each tub at a 'place'. One locomotive was retained at the shed as a 'spare' whilst one was usually under repair or being serviced.

On leaving the quarry on a right-hand curve, the trains of 'fulls' descended a slight gradient before crossing the Hampeth Burn. After the burn the gradient was against the engine as the train passed through a small copse and over a cattle grid. The line then crossed over an open field, staying close to the hedgerow and fence, and a second cattle grid. The upward gradient continued until the arrival at the works yard.

In 1966 the county council decided to lay a roadway to the quarry. This led ultimately to the closure of the rail system. However, railway operations continued until after mid-July 1968 when photographs were taken at the quarry. It was in 1969 that Thomas Ward of Sheffield acquired all seven of the locomotives, the rolling stock and the trackwork for scrap. This was all removed from Hare Crag in May 1969. All of the plant at the works site was demolished. After the brief reopening of the quarry in the 1970s, and until the start of the 21st century, the Hare Crag site became a civic amenity site, where the people of Alnwick and its surroundings could leave waste material for recycling or for landfill. Today the site of the quarry can be barely discerned on the hillside and the amenity site has been replaced by another closer to Alnwick. The works site and the former route of the railway to the quarry lie on private land and permission must be sought to make a visit. However, there is little to be gained from visiting the site today.

19 – The Breamish Gravel Works Railway near Powburn

The River Breamish arises in the Cheviot Hills. It is an important tributary of the River Till, which, in turn, flows into the River Tweed. Between the villages of Brandon and Branton there is a substantial terrace or floodplain 'with deposits of sand and gravel underlain by rocks of the Cementstone Group of the Lower Carboniferous series'. These deposits, easily reachable, have been an important source of stone for roadmaking for the Highways Department of Northumberland County Council.

The records of gravel and sand extraction at this site (initially NU055169) that are held by the county council, are incomplete and the precise date of the start of work appears to have been lost in history. The site was, however, leased from Guy Hunter Allwood, the owner of the estate, and deliveries of rails appear to have started in May 1924 and carried on until 1925 when Robert Hudson & Co.

This aerial photograph, taken in the late 1950s, shows the County Council Works at Powburn. Close examination reveals some of the lines, tipper wagons and the elevators leading to the screens. The A697 Morpeth to Wooler Road is on the right with the River Breamish at the top of the picture.

Michael Fairnington Collection

supplied some three-way turnouts. New conveyor belts were purchased in 1927, the same year as two new sheds to cover the plant and protect it from the effects of the weather. A new hydraulic washing machine with a 9 hp engine was supplied in 1928. In 1931 new steel hoppers were delivered, also a new screen and screenplates. In 1932, twenty-four elevator buckets came from the Ewart Chainbelt Co. The site operated successfully, though complaints were received from local fishermen concerned about the amount of sand being washed into the river, which was having a marked affect on the fish stocks! The local fishermen were finally paid £50 for the damage to the 'fishings' on the Carr-Ellison Estate, downstream of the works.

The original county council lease was renewed in 1929 and in 1949. The county council operated a 2 ft gauge railway at the site until the early 1960s, the last piece of track being lifted in 1964. The locomotives and wagons were then scrapped, or moved for further use elsewhere, and road vehicles started to bring the stone and gravel from the river terraces. After some financial operating losses in the 1970s the county council interests were transferred to Northern Aggregates of Yarm, Cleveland, part of the Readymix Concrete Group; they expanded the site and installed a new weighbridge for their road vehicles. In 1990 the company received a 'Sand and Gravel Restoration Award' for the recovery and restoration of 28 acres of the Breamish Valley site. This scheme involved much landscaping and tree-planting.

Stone extraction commenced, in the 1920s, quite close to the Works which was located close to the main Morpeth to Wooler road (now the A697), with the railway just a few hundred yards in length. Later as the site of extraction moved towards the west, so the railway was extended until it was between ¾ mile and 1 mile in length. The 'main line' was known as 'the marsh line'. At the far end of the site was the loading area. Loading was done by men using picks and pointed spades or shovels. They often worked in teams of six or eight men. The wagons used were 'triangular in section' (V-shaped side-tippers) and ran on the narrow-gauge rails. At the river terrace loading area were located several sidings, some containing the wagons being loaded, some containing either 'fulls' or further empty wagons. These sidings could be shifted whenever it was necessary for movement to a new loading site when the supply of stone became exhausted at the original one, when the river changed its course or when heavy rain caused some of the workings to become flooded.

Retired quarryman, Alan Voutt, MBE, recalls that the 'fulls', in trains of about six wagons, were propelled along the 'marsh line', on the south side of the river, by one of the locomotive fleet. Empties were often hauled in rakes of up to 10 wagons. One of the main drivers was a certain Eric Thompson who was never seen without a rakishly-angled cloth cap and a cigarette in the corner of his mouth! Propelling the wagons along the line and up some of the short gradients made the locomotives work hard! As the line approached the Works there was a short line leading off to the locomotive shed. Here, the locomotive fuel was kept in two separate tanks, one for diesel and one for petrol. The train would be propelled around a left-hand curve before the wagons' contents, after weighing, were deposited in the 'feeding-in hole', which led the stone, via elevated buckets and conveyors, to the crushing plant and screens. These conveyors

Between Brandon and Powburn there are extensive river terraces of stone and gravel which provided the stone for the County Council works at the site. This view was taken from the new footbridge over the Breamish at Brandon and shows one of the terraces that was 'quarried'.
Author

Petrol-engined Motor Rail locomotive No. 1217 worked at Powburn between 1963 and 1969. Its sole function was to 'bump start' the diesel locomotive, HE2834, each morning at the start of the shift. It was later transferred from Powburn to Hare Crag Quarry where this photograph was taken. Photos of locomotives working at Powburn have proved elusive!   *Dr C.G. Down*

were driven by a coal-fired Fowler traction engine (believed to have been nicknamed 'Bessie'), under the supervision of Bob Little, which was permanently sited in a small black corrugated iron shed. Coal was brought to the site by local hauliers John Lee & Sons. The crushers were originally powered by a Ransomes, Sims & Jeffries boiler, which was under the supervision of the works manager, Jimmy Ruff. A large water tank was the reservoir for the engine's water supply. Later the Ransomes boiler was replaced by an electric motor. The crushers themselves were made by Baxter's of Leeds; they had a patent 'knapping action' to reduce the size of the gravel to a useable size. Gravel was sorted by the screens into different sizes, such as '½ inch' or '¾ inch'.

Nearby were located several sidings for the emptied wagons and also one leading to the wagon weighbridge. Another line led across a wooden trestle bridge, standing on concrete footings, over the Breamish to a sand tip located to the north side of the river. A pair of further lines served 'the silt pond' (silt was derived from the washing process), and the 'sand hole'. Gravel was often stockpiled at the Works and the crushed stone was tipped into a pile using the tipper wagons. From time to time the level of the siding next to the stockpile had to be raised so that the edges of the piles did not cover the track. When there was a large demand for road gravel some was loaded by means of a conveyor onto side-tipping road lorries. Some loads were taken directly to where they were needed, both in county council lorries and in those owned by local haulage contractors, such as Scott's of Wooler, the Grant Brothers of Brandon, or John Lee & Sons of Lilburn. Generally these loads were laid as a top-dressing on freshly laid macadam. Other loads were taken to nearby Hedgeley station where the stone was transferred, in the small goods yard, to the LNER. Up to 10 or 12 empty wagons would arrive on the local Alnwick to Wooler pick-up goods train. These wagons had a capacity to hold 10 tons of stone and were loaded from an elevated ramp from which the lorries could tip their loads. The station yard was located just a short distance along the main road from the Works. On the corner by the yard entrance were several slot machines where the workers, of both quarry and railway, could replenish their supply of 'Beech Nut' chewing gum (two packets for 1d.) and 'Woodbine' cigarettes (a packet of five for 2d.). (Some of this information was provided by John Facer, whose uncle was the porter-signalman at the station and who supervised the loading process.)

The records of the amounts of stone taken away from the Works between the 1920s and the early 1940s appear not to have survived. However, in 1948 some 25,000 tons were taken away. In the mid-1960s the amount varied between 50,000 and 62,500 tons per year. The annual profit was between £2,000 and £11,000.

Five small locomotives are known to have worked at the Powburn site by the River Breamish; each had a mechanical transmission. Four were petrol-engined machines, one had a diesel engine.

All four of the petrol-engined Simplex locomotives have been identified. One of the first to arrive was MR1217 (built in 1918) which arrived from Closehead Quarry, near Otterburn. This eventually found its way to Hare Crag Quarry near Shilbottle, when the Powburn line closed in the 1960s. The second was MR1222/1918 which came to Powburn after working at Glendue Quarry near

After closure of the works the plant was demolished and sold or scrapped. Some of the rails were purchased for reuse, though not on a railway! Here, adjacent to the Ingram Valley road, some rails have found alternative employment as part of a cattle grid which replaces a field gate.
Author

This is a view of the River Breamish from the A697 road bridge, which would be almost idyllic if not for the lengths of rail projecting from the river bank and from the river bed. Other rail lengths are visible in the river when the water level is low.   *Author*

Hexham. Its subsequent fate is not known. The third, MR1225/1918, was moved 'up the road' from Moor House Quarry when it closed at the end of the 1920s. All of these had formerly been War Department Light Railway locomotives. The fourth was MR3687 which was brand new when it arrived at Powburn, a £475 quote for its supply being accepted by the county council. It later moved to Hare Crag. The fifth engine was HE2834 which was built in 1944. It was equipped with an 'Ailsa Craig' type engine of about 20 hp and was notoriously difficult to start. It arrived at Powburn after a brief period of ownership by the Ministry of Supply. This locomotive was also later transferred to Hare Crag Quarry, for further use, along with MR1217. These two locomotives were the last ones to work at Powburn and are remembered clearly by Alan Voutt. He recalls that if both locomotives had been at work then it was always the petrol engined-one that was placed in the small shed first at the end of the day! Its first job, at the start of the next day, was to 'bump start' the cab-fitted Hunslet-built diesel machine The petrol-engined locomotive was easy to start with a hand crank, and, after pushing the diesel to start its engine, would then be returned to its place in the shed if not required for other work! Minor servicing was performed at Powburn by the local staff. When a locomotive need something more complex, such as a major overhaul, a workman was sent to the Powburn works from Morpeth. The shed was located at the opposite end of the building which formed the workers' mess room, locally referred to as the 'bait cabin'. The gentlemen's conveniences were a short distance away, being located between the works and the river!

An old, long-out-of-use, steam-hammer was located not far from the gravel sidings, whilst adjacent to the gravel works site was an old aircraft hangar where large pre-cast spans were made for bridges. Its operations were quite separate from those of the county council.

The site of the former crushers and loaders at the works is now hidden by trees and shrubs and much of the riverside area has been landscaped. The former works site is on private land; however there are no remains worth seeing. The route of the river has shifted slightly since the 1920s and 1930s and a new bridge has replaced the former steel girder bridge on the main road by the site. The former NER/LNER, later British Railways', line and sidings were closed and lifted many years ago, though much of the trackbed and several features, including Hedgeley station (in private ownership) and bridge abutments, survive. In the vicinity several 'relics' of the old gravel works railway survive, purchased, after its closure, by local farmers. For example several lengths of rail are in use as fence posts and others have been used to make cattle grids at the entrance to fields near Brandon. Some rails can be spied, when water levels are low, on the bed of the River Breamish, and others project from the riverbank or bed, for example just above the A697 road bridge. A good view of the river terraces with their still-extensive reserves of stones and gravel can be seen from the footbridge which crosses the river close to the site of the former ford near to Brandon village on the Ingram Valley road.

Above: This general view of Ward's Hill Quarry shows the sloping rock layers with the quarry's lowest level on the right-hand side. A steep incline leads up to the higher quarry level on the left-hand side. This incline was locomotive worked.

Author

Right: At the side of the former cable-hauled incline, linking the quarry's upper level with the roadside, lie pieces of lightweight, old, quarry rails with the bolt holes for their fishplates still evident despite considerable rusting.

Author

Chapter Seven

The Quarry Railways near to Rothbury

Three quarry railways near to Rothbury are known to have employed railways for moving their stone. Those at Ward's Hill, Forestburngate and Ewesley are located to the south-east or south of Rothbury, whilst that at Biddlestone lay at the edge of the Coquet Valley to the north-west. Their railways were very different! That at Wards Hill was of narrow gauge and employed diesel locomotives. At Forestburngate and at Ewesley the lines were of standard gauge and steam locomotives were used. The fourth line, at Biddlestone, was a self-acting cableway on a steep gradient.

20 - The Ward's Hill Whinstone Quarry Railway

Ward's Hill is found about two miles south west of Pauperhaugh bridge (near the B6334, Rothbury to Weldon Bridge road) and half a mile east of the B6342 at Forestburn Gate.

It was in the second decade of the 20th century that whinstone quarrying commenced on Ward's Hill. Two quarries were developed: one was immediately to the side of the present Wardshill Cottage (NZ 083970) and the other was a few hundred yards along the road to the south-west (NZ079965). The former was a small quarry and was worked for a few years only. As far as is known there was no railway in this quarry, road vehicles being loaded directly. The second quarry, also to the east of the road, was similarly small until it was taken over by W.T. Bathgate Ltd.

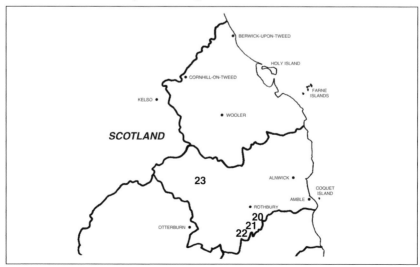

This is a panoramic view of the upper level at Ward's Hill Quarry with, in the foreground, the alignment of the former cable-hauled incline leading up to the roadside. Until recently there were the remains of the former rollers over which the cable passed; these have now disappeared.
Author

This huge block of concrete is the remains of the base of the haulage engine which formerly brought up wagons of stone from the upper level of the quarry shown in a previous picture. All of the other plant at this location was removed when the quarry closed in the 1960s.   *Author*

The owner of the company was W.T. ('Willy') Bathgate who is perhaps better known locally for being the operator of the Greenleighton Quarry & Limeworks near Netherwitton. Willy Bathgate took over the quarry at Ward's Hill shortly after the end of World War II and extracted whinstone until the early 1960s when he sold out to the Tilcon company. The quarry closed soon afterwards. The first stone to be removed came from the part of the quarry close to the road. However, the layers of whinstone sloped markedly towards the east and to continue extraction it was necessary for the quarry to become much deeper as excavations continued. The quantity of overburden increased thus increasing the cost of the quarrying. Adjacent to the nearby road a crushing and screening plant was set up to reduce the stone to a size suitable for roadstone which was its principal use.

To raise the stone from the quarry a small narrow gauge railway (marked 'Tramway' on some maps) was built and a winch was used to haul the loaded wagons, attached to a cable, from the loading points close to the quarry faces. Rotating drums between the rails guided the cables around the slight curves and over changes in gradient. As the stone in the first part of the quarry became exhausted it was necessary to move the face towards the south and east and to extend the railway system. So as to raise the laden wagons from the new lower level, Bathgate arranged for the transfer of two 'spare' locomotives from his Greenleighton site to Ward's Hill. This occurred in the 1950s. The two locomotives were small 2 ft gauge Ruston & Hornsby 4-wheeled diesel-

This is the last of the quarry faces to have been worked by Bathgate's at Ward's Hill Quarry. The stone face is several metres deep at this point whereas in other parts of the quarry it is more shallow and there is an overburden of friable rock.   *Author*

mechanical machines. The first was the oldest of the Greenleighton 'fleet', with Works No. RH195844; it was built in 1939 and had been purchased new for use there. The second was a similar locomotive, number RH235653, built in 1946. Their role was to propel the loaded wagons from the lower parts of the quarry to the intermediate level where the cable could be attached for raising them to the crushers. Their years of operation at Ward's Hill were limited, the first locomotive being transferred back to Greenleighton in about 1962; the other was scrapped, apparently on site, in 1969. Normally one locomotive was in use, the other being kept 'spare'. No shed was provided to shelter the locomotives. Instead a tarpaulin covered them to give protection when the locomotives were not working. Any minor repairs needed were performed on site.

Bathgate's interests at Ward's Hill were later taken over by the Tilcon company though their records do not show whether they excavated much stone.

The Ward's Hill area quarries can be inspected if due care is shown. Access to the quarries is easy from the nearby road and there is plenty of space to park a car safely. (One must beware of the cattle which are allowed to roam free in this vicinity. They seem to have a liking for rubbing themselves against car wing mirrors!) Within the whinstone quarry some lengths of old rail can still be found and the inclines connecting the various levels are still evident. The concrete remains visible at the roadside are, according to Thompson Bathgate, son of Willy, the remains of the base of the haulage drum for the cable-worked upper incline. The quarry faces reveal bands of whinstone and coal.

Towards the lowest level of Ward's Hill Quarry is this huge concrete block with some fixing bolts protruding. It is reputed to be the base of Bathgate's crane which was used for loading stone into the quarry wagons. The superstructure was removed when the quarry closed in the 1960s. *Author*

21 - The Forestburn Quarry Railway

Forestburn Colliery (NZ 076968) and the nearby Forestburn Quarry (NZ 076966) were linked to the North British Railway's Scots Gap to Rothbury branch by a ¾ mile-long standard gauge mineral railway. The colliery and quarry were located in Ravens Cleugh which is in the valley of the Forest Burn. The sites, just a couple of hundred yards apart, were about 12½ miles south-south-west of Alnwick, not far from the Rothbury to Scots Gap road. The full story of the colliery railway appeared in Volume Two but brief details of the use of the line for stone transport can be included here.

In March 1921 the Northumberland Collieries Ltd took over the colliery and quarry. Later, a concern called the Northumberland Quarries Ltd took coal and stone from the site, probably still making use of the railway. This last company was never registered and may have been simply a convenient 'trading name'. Though quantities of stone were removed from the quarry by rail, records of its destination and use appears not to have survived.

Stone wagon 'empties' were left in the loop, which was about 150 yards in length, by the NBR/LNER branch locomotive, and full wagons of stone were collected from the same point. Whereas coal empties were propelled along the line by the company locomotive named *Wingate* (Works No. AB675/1891), it was necessary to haul empty stone wagons to beyond the trailing junction for the quarry siding. From this point the wagons would be propelled into the quarry. The quarry branch, like the line to the colliery, was single tracked and maps show no further sidings in the quarry itself. From its junction with the

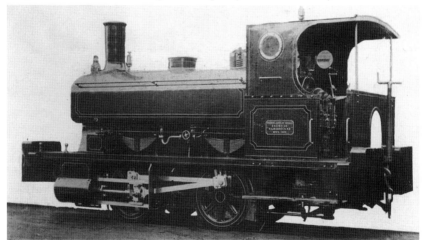

This view of saddle tank *Wingate* (Works No. AB 675/1891) is the only photograph I have been able to trace which relates to the Forestburn system and, as such, it also appears in Volume Two alongside the entry for the Forestburn Colliery Railway. *Wingate* continued to work for Northumberland Quarries Ltd serving their Forestburngate Quarry after the nearby Forestburngate Colliery had closed in 1924.

University of Glasgow/Andrew Barclay Archive

Fortunately a photograph of the interior of Ewesley Quarry was taken, for geological purposes, whilst its railway was still operational. On the right are two wagons (one bearing the letters LMS) partly laden with crushed stone. A second siding lies on the left of the picture and remains can be discerned of some narrow gauge wagons including a grounded tipper body.

British Geological Survey

The Ewesley Quarry employed three standard gauge steam locomotives. This is their *Ewesley* No. 2 (HL 2496/1901) which came new to the quarry and worked there until just before World War II. Note the huge buffers and the jack standing on the buffer beam!   *Author's Collection*

colliery line it headed approximately 300 yards southwards into the quarry, crossing over the Forest Burn by a small bridge en route. It has not been possible to discover the details of any plant used in the quarry, the amount of stone extracted, or to discover how many men were employed there. It is possible that men worked either at the colliery or at the quarry 'as required'.

Loaded wagons of stone were hauled from the quarry siding to beyond the junction with the colliery line and then propelled up to the loop adjacent to the Rothbury branch awaiting collection by the branch goods train. It is believed that the quarry continued to function after the cessation of mining at the colliery in 1923 and the locomotive may have still functioned until towards the end of the decade. This must have been uneconomic and probably hastened the demise of the quarry. The locomotive is known to have been employed elsewhere by the middle of 1930.

Today the former quarry site is surrounded by trees and there is little of interest to see. It lies on private land but permission to visit it can be obtained from the nearby farm. This involves crossing fields which may contain livestock.

22 - The Ewesley Quarry Railways

Ewesley Quarry (NZ 061942) is situated some six miles south of Rothbury and 14½ miles south-west of Alnwick. Its entrance is some 450 yards to the east of the White House Limestone Quarry and about 1¼ miles to the east of the former Fontburn station. It was a whinstone quarry yielding a good quality igneous stone. Between the turn of the century and about 1908 it was operated by the Ewesley Quarry Co. and used as a source of the stone associated with the building of the nearby Fontburn Reservoir. In 1910 its production switched to roadstone, with stone being supplied, for example, for the building of the 'Morpeth to Shields road'. In 1911 further stone was supplied for the same road, together with chippings for the 'Holystone to Earsdon road'. In 1914 stone was supplied for repairs to roads at Forestburn, Lordingshaw, Whitton Burn, Thropton and Hartburn, and whinstone setts were supplied to Ashington District Council. There was little quarry activity during the war. From the period after World War I there are records of stone chippings being supplied by rail to Meldon station for Morpeth Rural District Council (1923) and for the Great North Road, which was being widened between Newcastle and Berwick (1925). This latter contract provided for the daily delivery of between 20 and 25 tons of crushed whinstone and chippings to Morpeth station. The county council paid 12s. per ton for this. The company also successfully tendered for the supply of tarred chippings to the county council during the following five years and in 1933 the county council accepted delivery of loads of Ewesley stone at their depot at Belsay. The Ewesley Quarry Co. continued to operate the quarries until 1950, though in later years the standard gauge line was abandoned and a narrow gauge rail system was used within the quarry to take stone to the elevator for the crushers and screens. Stone then left the quarry by road until the 1960s with several local firms including Telfers (of nearby Cambo) and W.T. Bathgate being involved. A brief period of closure followed.

Taken in the early 1960s this photograph illustrates the period when W.T. ('Willy') Bathgate was taking stone from Ewesley. The picture shows Bathgate's excavator loading a portable crusher which feeds crushed stone into one of Bathgate's lorries. *Jack Hall*

J.R.M. Telfer & Sons of Scots Gap also obtained stone from Ewesley. Driver Jack Hall's Seddon lorry is filled with crushed stone, for local delivery, by an International tractor fitted with caterpillar tracks. *Jack Hall*

By the 1970s the Thomas Tilling Group operated at the quarries, though without a rail system, and the TILCON name appeared on the sides of the road vehicles. The main product was still chippings for roads. Today the quarry is disused and gated, though some agricultural plant has been stored undercover within the quarry.

The first rail line from the quarry, from about 1895 onwards, may well have been a horse-drawn narrow gauge line linking the quarry with the side of the Rothbury branch. Alan Renton, who farmed the land until recently, reported the former existence of a narrow embankment leading from the quarry and crossing the 'rigg and furrow' pattern in the nearby fields. This caused him some difficulty when ploughing the land. The line also crossed over a farm track. No documentary evidence has come to light concerning the nature and operation of this early, probably short-lived, narrow gauge line.

In the days of the Ewesley Quarry Co. much of the stone left the quarry via the company's own mineral railway, which was almost a mile in length. It was laid to the standard gauge (4 ft 8½ in.) and opened just after the start of the 20th century. It served the various quarry faces, the OS map of 1926 showing a 'fan' of five lines distributed throughout the quarry. The line left the quarry entrance in a south-easterly direction and a line, continuing in this direction, led to a spoil tip. The 'main line' curved sharply towards the west, following the contour for about a third of its length. Then it started to descend and its alignment cut through the embankment of the former White House Quarry's tramway (see later volume). Its gradient became steeper and its direction became more north-westerly as it approached the former limeworks sidings. At the sidings it joined the most easterly line (though later the other sidings would be removed). This allowed a direct connection with the Rothbury branch. On the ground evidence suggests that a small siding trailed in from the limestone quarry shortly before the line cut through the older limestone quarry tramway's route. It has not been possible to discover any documentary evidence relating to the use of this siding. Perhaps some stone or rubble was removed from the limestone quarry by standard gauge wagons after its former tramway was closed.

The Ewesley Quarry Co. owned three steam locomotives which were used on the quarry system. The first locomotive was named *Ewesley No. 1*. It was a tiny outside-cylindered 0-4-0 saddle tank with 2 ft 9 in. wheels. Its cylinder dimensions were 9 in. diameter by 14 in. stroke. It was built by the Leeds firm of Manning, Wardle and its works number was MW495/1874. It first worked for the Strafford Colliery Co. near Barnsley in Yorkshire. It was sent to the Hudswell, Clarke works when it needed an overhaul in 1898. After the necessary work had been completed they hired it out for a couple of jobs. The Ewesley company purchased it in 1900 or 1901 from the engineering machinery merchants R.H. Longbotham of Wakefield, who had previously bought it from Hudswell, Clarke. Nothing is known of its history after it finished working at Ewesley.

The second locomotive to arrive at the quarry was, not surprisingly, named *Ewesley No. 2*. This was a Hawthorn, Leslie-built 0-4-0 saddle tank with works number HL2496/1901. It had 12 in. x 18 in. outside cylinders. It was new when it came to Ewesley but around 1939 it was sold to Steel's Engineering Products Ltd, of Crown Works in Sunderland. It was subsequently at Sir Hedworth

Above: This view of the entrance to Ewesley Quarry was photographed, with permission, in 2009. The quarry is now used for the grazing of livestock whilst the building located in the centre is used for the storage of farm machinery. Some fragments of dumped rail are still visible embedded in the banks at the entrance to the quarry.

Author

Right: The approach to the Rothbury branch from the Ewesley Quarry railway was via a steep incline. Photographed in 2009 this view shows surviving wooden sleepers on this incline. The trees in the distance mark the level crossing with the alignment of the former tramway line linking Ritton Whitehouse limestone quarry with the lime kilns.

Author

Williamson's Limeworks at Fulwell, where it was named *Nicholas*. (One record has the locomotive at Short Brothers, Pallion, for a time.)

The third Ewesley locomotive also arrived new. This was an Andrew Barclay 0-4-0 saddle tank (Works No. AB1250/1911) and was identified as *Ewesley No. 3*, or perhaps simply '3', in the company's lists. It had 10 in. x 18 in. outside cylinders and wheels of 3 ft 0½ in. diameter. It was scrapped sometime after January 1938 after lying in a siding at Ewesley awaiting disposal. The use of steam locomotives at the quarry thus ceased prior to World War II.

One archive photograph which dates from the late 1920s shows the standard gauge sidings within the quarry and an LMS open wagon filled with crushed stone. One other item of interest in the photograph is a narrow gauge side-tipper wagon which appears to be on a short length of track. This wagon is also stone filled, which suggests that there may have been a narrow gauge network within the quarry at this time, perhaps for conveying stone from the faces to the crushers. Alternatively the wagons may be relics of the possible narrow gauge line referred to earlier.

A small 2 ft gauge system was certainly laid within the quarry in the early 1950s and conveyed stone from the quarry faces to the elevator, which led stone to the crushers and screens. It employed a single locomotive which did not carry a running number. It was built by the Motor Rail as works number MR8614 of 1941. It arrived at Ewesley, after War Department use, during 1951 and had a working life of about 10 years there, being sold to G. Foster of Ramshaw Fluorspar Mine, Ramshaw, County Durham around 1962. Its use was presumably intermittent for in 1952 visitors reported the locomotive as out of use and looking derelict. The narrow gauge system was later lifted and all subsequent movement of stone, both within and from the quarry, was by road vehicles. (The Ramshaw mine closed in about 1962 but the locomotive remained on site stored in a shed along with about 12 tipper wagons. Its subsequent fate is not known.)

In the 1920s Ritton Whitehouse Farm was very important in the lives of many of the Ewesley quarrymen and their families. The farmhouse was occupied by the quarry manager, Mr Smith, and others. Its converted outbuildings provided living accommodation for over 100 individuals, including the 'bothy' which housed mainly Irish navvies. There was also a canteen (the 'Club'), a Mission Hut and two rows of huts known as 'Cockney Row' and the' Black Huts'.

Today these sites can only be approached via a public footpath which follows the private road from the B6342. Ewesley Quarry is gated and permission must be sought from the landowner to inspect it. Some lengths of old rail project from a bank just outside the quarry entrance. Part of the former standard gauge trackbed towards the sidings at Fontburn now forms the rather rough access road to the White House farm complex, and to the cottages, now called 'Daisy Cottages', adjacent to the site of the former Fontburn station. These cottages are occupied dwellings and access to them involves crossing private land. A recently built extension to Daisy Cottages resembles a railway signal box in outline! An alternative means of access to the sites is via a track from the water treatment works of Northumbrian Water at Fontburn. Once again this is on private land and permission to cross it must be sought from Northumbrian Water. These routes are marked on the latest OS maps.

23 – *The Biddlestone Quarry Railway in the Coquet Valley*

Visitors approaching Alwinton from the direction of the village of Netherton, in the Upper Coquet Valley, cannot fail to notice the large Harden Quarry at Biddlestone, a mile or so to their right. This quarry produces a unique and very distinctive red stone, usually referred to as 'Harden Red' often used as a decorative topping for tarmacadam. Geologically it is 'a mica-porphyritic type of granite'. Parts of the A1 and other local roads, the hard shoulders of the M2 and the forecourt of Buckingham Palace and The Mall in London are all dressed with this stone. This quarry first opened in the second half of the 20th century.

Before the opening of the large Harden Quarry the much smaller Biddlestone Quarry existed nearby. It was located to the east of Harden Quarry and lower down on the valley side (NT962084). This quarry was opened by a local firm, Brydens of Otterburn in about 1926. Later, in the early 1930s, it was taken over by the Limmer & Trinidad Lake Asphalt Co. It was this second company that constructed and used a quarry railway here in 1938. The line led from the quarry down the hillside towards Biddlestone Town Foot.

The quarry relied heavily on manpower. The stone was extracted with picks and loaded into the railway wagons using shovels. The wagons could accommodate upwards of 30 hundredweight of stone. The railway system was some 300 yards long and took the form of a self-acting inclined plane. There were two parallel tracks with two wagons or 'tubs' on each line. The tubs were of the four-wheeled side-tipper type and V-shaped in section, though their maker is not known. The two pairs of coupled wagons were linked by a steel cable which passed around a braked wheel at the upper end of the line at the quarry. There were no spare wagons. The gauge of the line was about 2 ft. The track was composed of flat-bottomed rail laid directly on wooden sleepers, there being one spike on each side of the rail on each sleeper.

The loaded wagons descended the gradient of about 1 in 7 by gravity, at the same time pulling the 'empties' up the gradient. At the lower end of the line there were no buffers, just transversely laid sleepers at the rail ends. The stone was tipped from the wagons onto a conveyor leading to the crushers. The crushed stone passed through a rotating screen which sorted the chippings into piles of various diameters: ⅜ in., ½ in. and ¾ in., being the main sizes. Some of the chippings were loaded into road vehicles for subsequent use as a road dressing whilst some were added to tar in the 'tar plant' which operated 'like a huge cement mixer' according to the former quarryman George ('Geordie') Hall who worked in the quarry.

Health & Safety regulations were much less stringent in those days and there were several accidents at the site. On one occasion a screen operator caught his foot on a protruding bolt and his clothing became caught in the rotating screen. He was pulled over the top of the screen and thrown down on the other side, fortunately without serious injury. However, the most dramatic accident took place when the steel cable joining the wagons parted when the descending 'fulls' had just passed the ascending 'empties'. The full wagons accelerated down the gradient, hit the sleepers at the bottom and flew through the air over the hedges of the nearby road and landed in the cow field opposite! The empties were prevented from following the same route by becoming tangled in the cable on the gradient.

The line continued in use throughout World War II but by 1946 it saw little use and was dismantled. Its brief existence meant that it did not feature on any Ordnance Survey maps. For a few years more small quantities of stone were removed using a mechanical excavator and lorries for transport within, and from, the quarry. Shortly afterwards this quarry was closed and filled in. Nothing remains at the Biddlestone Quarry site today.

The Limmer & Trinidad company became part of the Tarmac Group in 1971. It is the Tarmac company which currently operates Harden Quarry, visible from miles around as a large red scar on the hillside, dominating this part of the Upper Coquet valley.

After the closure of the self-acting incline at Biddlestone Quarry all stone was removed directly from the quarry by road vehicles. One of local contractor J.R.M. Telfer & Sons' Seddon lorries is shown here being loaded with stone and fine rubble by an excavator.

Jack Hall

Chapter Eight

The Blaxter Quarry Tramway, Railway and Craneway

The Blaxter Quarry (NY933901) is located on Hunterlee Hill in the middle of Raylees Common, due south of the village of Elsdon in Redesdale. In the past it was also known as Elsdon Quarry. It lies some 16 miles north-north-west of Hexham and 3½ miles south-east of Otterburn, being located to the west of the Newcastle to Otterburn road (now the A696). The quarry only just falls within the Alnwick District Council area. Its name is derived from the surrounding area of former common land known as 'Black Stur'. It lies in a very exposed position at an altitude of 1,000 ft; the land is drained to the north and east by tributaries of the Raylees Burn, to the west and south by the Black Burn. Lying on the estate of the Swinburne family of Capheaton, it is a source of fine quality sandstone (freestone), buff or greyish in colour, formed in the Lower Carboniferous era. Blaxter stone is straightforward to cut and quarry and has therefore been in demand over a long period. It has, for example, been used in the construction of many elegant buildings in the north of England, such as St. Mary's College, Durham, also in Dublin, and in Princes Street, Lothian Road and surrounding streets in Edinburgh ('Edinburgh New Town'). It was also used during the building of the National Library of Scotland in 1937, and the Royal Museum of Scotland in 1958. Some Blaxter stone was used as facing stone during the construction of the Fontburn viaduct on the North British Railway's Rothbury branch. Recently Blaxter stone has been used in the rebuilding of Lancing College Chapel, the construction of the Edinburgh Mosque (1997; the value of the stone used was £250,000) and the 'Pitcher and Piano' building on the Newcastle Quayside (1994; the value of the stone used was £100,000). Other buildings recently repaired using Blaxter stone include Bishop Auckland town hall and the House of Fraser store ('Jenners') in Edinburgh.

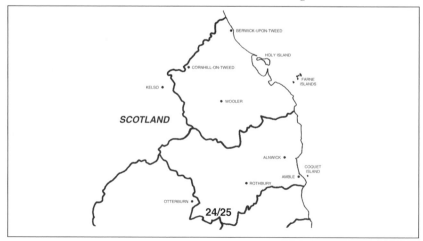

136

A small coal pit was located to the north of the quarry which was in occasional use from the mid-1800s to the early 1900s. Little has been discovered of its operation.

24 – The Blaxter Quarry Tramway

Blaxter Quarry was in use in, or before 1860, though at this time it was small and produced only a small quantity of stone for local use, this being transported away by horse-drawn cart. A cart track linked the quarry with the nearby road. However the censuses of 1861, 1871 and 1881 do not list anyone resident in the immediate area who listed their main occupation as quarrying.

The first discovered documentary evidence of named individuals being associated with the quarry dates from the early 1890s. In 1892 the Swinburne Estate leased an area of 10 acres, including the 'old quarry', to 'Messrs Reed and Minto'. Nicholas White Reed lived in Bath Lane Terrace, Newcastle and Andrew Steven Minto was resident in St Nicholas Buildings, Newcastle. Their rent was 10d. per ton for stone removed from the quarry and 3d. per ton for rubble. In 1892 they removed 92 tons and 17 cwt of grindstones and 176 tons 9 cwt of building stone. On 14th November, 1893 a surviving document drawn up by the solicitors, Gascoignes of Newcastle, offers Thomas Gow of Cambo the whole of the Blaxter Quarry from the 'Newcastle Grinding Company'. It is

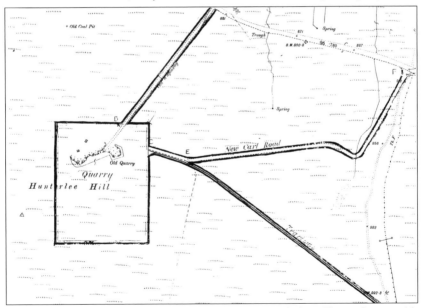

This map marks both the new rail line, marked 'Tramway' linking Blaxter Quarry with Knowesgate station and the earlier line, marked 'Old Waggonway', which linked the quarry with the nearby Newcastle to Otterburn road.   *Northumberland Record Office*

likely, in view of the evidence above, that the Newcastle Grinding Co. was the trading name of Reed and Minto, and that they were trying to sub-let the working of the quarry to Gow. However, Reed became bankrupt by 1895 and the lease was surrendered. It was on the 12th November, 1896 that a further lease agreement was drawn up between Sir John Swinburne of Capheaton Hall and James Watson of Whitburn Terrace, Marsden, for 'Blaxter Quarry on the farm Ravenscleugh' As well as quarrying rights it granted permission for the erection of a tramway over a portion of the farm to 'the public road from Kirkwhelpington to Otterburn' for the purpose of carrying away the produce of the quarry. The quarry was stated to be 'of ten acres' at that time. The lease was to last for 15 years at a rent of £20 per annum, to increase by an additional £10 later.

The Ordnance Survey map, reflecting the survey conducted in the 1890s, shows that a single-track tramway had been constructed linking the quarry to the road. The gauge of the line is not known. It was about 400 yards in length and allowed stone to be moved on rail wagons to the roadside at a point about 850 feet above Ordnance Datum. The lie of the land allowed loaded wagons to descend using gravity though it is likely that horses would have been needed to return the empties to the quarry. The 1890s map marks the tramway as 'Disused'.

Watson was still the lessee in 1899. Details of the amount of stone quarried are sparse. However, in March 1902 between five and eight tons per day were being won with a total of 15 days worked in the month.

25 – The Blaxter Quarry Railways and Craneway

On 12th May, 1904 a new lease for the quarry was negotiated by Watson, this time in a partnership involving John Wright Johnson, a colliery agent of Sunderland, and William George Browell, a builder, also of Sunderland. The lease referred to the land, *two* tramways and a road. The partnership's registered office was at 24 Foyle Street in Sunderland, with the quarry's address being recorded as the Blaxter Freestone Quarry, Elsdon. In the company's early years some of the stone was sold locally: for example in the year from the start of May 1906 to the start of May 1907 93¾ tons of stone and 7½ tons of rubble were delivered by horse and cart. However, it is clear that much of the stone and rubble was being transported further afield, for a letter of 15th January, 1906 refers to the damage being caused to local roads by 'Blaxters' when hauling their stone by traction engine to Knowesgate Quarry and to Ponteland. The county council informed Blaxters that they would effect the road repairs but that the cost would be charged to Blaxters. Probably it was this that stimulated Blaxters into the planning and construction of a railway line to link their quarry with Knowesgate railway station on the North British Railway. Having their own railway would, hopefully, eliminate the need for the company to make contributions to future road repairs, which were predicted as being likely in view of the fact that the foundations of the road were upon spongy moorland with clay beneath.

The railway line was constructed between 1907 and 1908 following the establishment of a new lease, this time referring to the partnership between Messrs Watson, Browell and Johnson as 'Blaxters Ltd'. The lease was for an extended period of 27 years at £30 per annum plus royalties on the stone and rubble extracted. It allowed for some disposal of stone locally and the installation of a 25 cwt weighing machine at the quarry to assist with this. Cottages were made available for the quarrymen at a rent of £1 per half year.

The line ran from the quarry to Knowesgate station alongside the Otterburn to Kirkwhelpington road. Its first locomotive was delivered in November 1908 and was a small Hudswell, Clarke & Co. 0-4-0 saddle tank with 8 in. x 12 in. cylinders. Its works number was HC418 and it was built in 1894. It was first employed a few miles away from Blaxter Quarry by the Newcastle and Gateshead Waterworks Department during the construction of their reservoir at Catcleugh in Redesdale, when it was named *Otterburn*. In July 1904 it had been bought by the Tynemouth Corporation for use during the building of their Fontburn Reservoir (q.v.) where it was renamed *Fontburn*. On its subsequent purchase by Blaxters its name was changed to *Ottercops* after a house in the locality of the quarry. A locomotive shed, to house the engine, was constructed at the quarry end of the line.

The line, of 3 ft gauge, left the quarry at a height of about 1,000 ft and descended the slopes of Hunterlee Hill towards the main road which it reached at a point about 3½ miles from Otterburn (as measured by the milestones alongside the road) at a height of about 906 ft. Following the roadside it ascended to a summit of around 1,020 ft where the track became level for a short distance before starting a descent to Ottercops Burn (855 ft). Another uphill

Knowesgate station, built by the North British Railway lay on the line between Scots Gap and Reedsmouth Junction stations. The sparse passenger trains used the track by the right-hand platform. The left-hand track functioned as a siding for wagons awaiting trans-shipment from the narrow gauge wagons of the Blaxter railway which ran onto the platform. The crane facilitated the unloading process.   *R.W. Lynn*

Locomotive HC418 bore the names *Otterburn* and *Fontburn* before arriving at Blaxter Quarry and being given the name *Ottercops* after the name of a nearby house. This is the works photograph taken soon after its manufacture in 1894.   *Author's Collection*

After briefly using a hired-in contractor's locomotive Blaxter Quarry took delivery of its second locomotive, namely HC 971, built in 1912. It was given the name *Blaxter*. Here, the locomotive, in almost new condition, is hauling a train of flat wagons for carrying large stone blocks.

Northumberland Record Office via Bill Sewell

gradient led to a second summit at the boundary of the Alnwick District on Kirkwhelpington Common (893 ft; approximately 6¼ miles from Otterburn). The line then commenced its final descent towards Knowesgate station (728 ft) passing the house called Raechester (825 ft) and the '8 miles to Otterburn' milepost at 754 ft. Parts of these gradients were severe. All heights are taken from the spot heights on the OS maps. As it approached Knowesgate station the line swung to the left passing the large house known as 'Knowes'. The line then ran parallel to the loop off the North British Railway's line from Scots Gap to Reedsmouth. Here, on the loading dock, there was a 5 ton crane for transferring the stone onto standard gauge wagons. The agreement for the construction of the line stipulated that the width of the trackbed should not exceed 15 ft including ditches, though this would have enabled passing loops to have been constructed if needed. The total length of the line was about 4½ miles and the building of the line involved the construction of several small bridges for the crossing of, for example, the Ravenscleugh, Ottercops and Fairnley burns.

Despite the construction and use of the railway, Blaxters continued to distribute some stone locally using a traction engine and horse-drawn carts (there being a road weighbridge at Knowesgate station). The road surface was once again being reported as 'breaking up' in places. In December 1911 Blaxters agreed to share the cost of repairs to the road between their quarry and Knowesgate with the county council. The reason for the county council meeting some of the cost was no doubt because they were receiving deliveries, by road, of Blaxter stone at their own Knowesgate Quarry! This quarry was being used as a depot for the supply and delivery of roadstone and other stone for council works in the local area. (A few years later the onset of World War I was to greatly increase the amount of heavy traffic over this road to the developing military facilities at both Otterburn and Redesdale Camps. At this time the repairs and improvements were jointly funded by the military authorities and the county council.)

On the 22nd July, 1910 there had been a fatal railway accident at the quarry. Robert Richardson, a 37-year-old wagon loader who came from Elsdon, was killed when he fell between wagons drawn by the locomotive *Ottercops*. This was the first of three reported fatalities at the quarry.

On 4th November, 1911 the company placed an advertisement in *Machinery Market* stating that they wished to hire, or to purchase, a 3 ft gauge locomotive.

Initially Blaxters hired a locomotive from the contractors, P. Drake & Sons. This locomotive has been identified as *Mary*, an outside-cylindered 0-4-0 saddle tank (Works No. WB1717 of 1903). It had been used by Drake's at Ogden Reservoir, Haslingden, Lancashire, and was originally advertised for sale there on 8th May, 1908. In 1910 it is recorded as having worked with the contractor H. Arnold during the construction of Embsay Reservoir near Skipton. This job was completed in October 1910. In the same month Drake's ordered spares for the locomotive but their name in the order book was deleted and that of 'Blaxter Quarries' substituted. This suggests that Blaxters hired this locomotive from Drake for a time, perhaps for up to two years, until their own second locomotive was delivered. (Further spares were ordered for the locomotive by Drake's in July 1911 but the delivery location is not recorded in the order book.) Notes

This photograph illustrates one of the Hudswell, Clarke locomotives at Blaxter Quarry, probably HC 971, though it is not identified on the back of the picture. It shows the locomotive in rather careworn state hauling a train of side-tipping wagons.   *Beamish Museum Collection*

This view of the inside of Blaxter Quarry shows a fixed crane on the right-hand side and a partially-tarpaulined delivery lorry, perhaps under repair. The nature and size of the stone blocks delivered from Blaxter can be appreciated in this view.

Northumberland Record Office via Bill Sewell

accompanying the photographs in the Charlton Collection at Beamish Museum refer to a locomotive named *May* being at Blaxter Quarry 'on hire'. This locomotive was probably the *Mary* referred to above.

It was in 1912 that the Blaxter Quarries Ltd took delivery of their own second, this time new, locomotive from the same builder as their first. It was a similar 0-4-0 saddle tank with the works number HC971. Its arrival both increased the amount of stone traffic moved over the line and reduced the need for movement of some stone by road. The locomotive bore the name *Blaxter*.

In 1914 the Blaxter company, for whom John Johnson was by now described as Managing Director, made the decision to diversify and open a coal mine close to their stone quarries. This may have been as a result of the commencement of the war and the downturn in stone demand. Accordingly an agreement was drawn up with the Swinburne Estate for a tramway to link the coal mine with the Hunter Lee Hill Quarry [*sic*] at a rental of £7 10s. per year from November 1914, additional sums being paid for each ton of coal won. It is not known how successful this mine was. In 1913, before the proposal to construct the tramway, just three men were working in the mine, coal being won from the 'Limestone Seam'.

In early 1915 the quarry was still producing 'High Class Architectural Freestone' at a rate of between 6 and 8½ tons per day, that is about six to twelve sawn blocks of stone. However, later in the year the quarry was closed and the railway was lifted soon afterwards. Some reports state that the rails were taken to France for further use on the military railways there. However, the Minutes of the Northumberland County Council Roads & Bridges Committee, dated 6th May, 1918, refer to Blaxters having sold their plant, but add that the War Office had commandeered their railway at the side of the road to Knowesgate. The War Office eventually considered it opportune to sell 825 yards of the rails. This rail amounted to some 30 tons which were sold at £30 per ton. These rails were bought and used by the Northumberland County Council at Closehead Quarry where a rail system, using a small 4-wheeled petrol locomotive (MR1217/1918), operated between 1919 and 1922 approximately. This locomotive subsequently worked at the Breamish Gravel Depot at Powburn (q.v.). Other rails were lifted by, and sold to, Messrs Holdsworth & Co.

The Blaxter steam locomotives were placed in store for two years and then offered for sale in an advertisement in the *Yorkshire Post* dated 22nd November, 1917. The subsequent fate of *Ottercops*, the older of the two is not confirmed. Some records suggest that it may have been sold or scrapped. However, Harold Bowtell, in his published work entitled *Dam Builders Railways* claims that the locomotive remained at Blaxter Quarry 'and ran as late as about 1947'. This would suggest that the locomotive failed to sell in 1917 and that it remained in the quarry even during the time when there was no narrow gauge system remaining (*see later*). However, it does not appear in inventories for the quarry dating from around 1930. The mystery remains.

The younger locomotive, *Blaxter*, was to perform more useful work. By 1920 (some sources say by the end of 1917) it had been sold to Lanarkshire County Council for use on the Camps Reservoir construction contract, three miles to the east of Crawford. It was disposed of on 28th July, 1930, around the time of the completion of the job, and it passed into the ownership of the contractor,

This photograph provides a glimpse of the start of the route towards Knowesgate after the closure of the rail line. The engine shed is shown on the left-hand side.

Beamish Museum Collection

This view of the locomotive shed at Blaxter Quarry, seen here housing a road vehicle some time after closure of the rail system, reveals a strongly-built structure, constructed using stone from the quarry. Originally it was fitted with stout wooden doors.   *Beamish Museum Collection*

Richard Baillie, of Haddington, south of Edinburgh. It worked on the Hopes Reservoir construction job for the East Lothian Water Board until 1935, and later, on the Ladybower Dam construction contract for Sheffield Corporation.

The county council Roads & Bridges Committee Minutes, dated 5th March, 1923, contain the following: 'The (Blaxter) freestone quarry was idle during the War and has now been reopened by Marshall and Company of Hawick.'

In the same Minutes, reference was made to their output having been transported by road, with there being no possibility of the building of a light railway until a steady market was established. Later the same month reference was made to the company entitled 'Blaxters Ltd', their registered office being 123 George Street, Edinburgh. (Perhaps this company was a trading name, or subsidiary, of Marshall's). They were described as a 'new' company taking a precarious risk in reopening the quarry, in view of likely rises in the costs of winning stone. It was considered that the cost of laying a new railway, whether 'narrow gauge or broad' could not be justified. It was recorded that the company wished to use a Foden lorry and trailer to move the stone. (It has been written elsewhere that they used two Sentinel road lorries.) Blaxters had said that the quarry was to be only a small one, producing, say, 15,000 tons per annum. They wished to lay a railway (presumably inside the quarry) at a cost of £6,000 and were prepared to pay £200 per year for the privilege of moving the stone over the local road up to a maximum of 10,000 tons, with 6*d*. per ton for any tonnage in excess of this figure. They wished to extract water from the Brimside Burn for their engine. By 1925 a total of 95 men was employed at the quarry.

A report of a second fatality at the quarry (in 1925) indicates that a craneway had been laid in the quarry. A quarry labourer was killed when he was crushed between the crane, with its jib trailing, on the craneway leading to the spoil tip, and a wagon it was hauling. The wind had gusted causing the jib to swing, knocking the man over. It was not known whether he had been standing beside the wagon or 'hitching a ride' on it. Nothing more has been discovered about this craneway, though some pictures of it survive.

By 28th February, 1927 it was reported that Blaxters had been transporting stone by road from their quarry to Knowesgate station for the trial period of three years (the agreement for the trial was dated 2nd August, 1923). (A photograph exists, which may date from this time, showing a lorry belonging to a carrier, a Mr Wilkinson, engaged in leading stone from Blaxter Quarry to Knowesgate.) No damage to the road was reported (perhaps as a result of the improvements made to the road almost 10 years earlier!). Blaxters were asked by the Roads & Bridges Committee if they had any plans to lay a railway from the quarry to Knowesgate. They received no reply to their question. During 1927 the quarry's third fatality took place, reported in the *Gazette* newspaper. A certain Ralph Dickenson of West Woodburn, died as a result of crush injuries to his head and stomach.

In 1927 the list of the company's assets contained no reference to a railway but in 1928 it was reported that the company had laid a standard gauge line within the quarry. Their railway purchases that year, including a new locomotive and wagons, amounted to £1,021 9*s*. 6*d*. An inventory of December 1928 indicated the ownership of the following items of railway equipment and materials:

Right: The hilltop position of the quarry is illustrated in this picture of Blaxter Quarry, taken probably in the 1920s when it is known that a crane operated on a craneway of standard gauge. It appears that the crane is about to lift one of the stone blocks in the foreground.

Northumberland Record Office via Bill Sewell

Below: In 1928 Blaxter Quarry purchased a new locomotive of an unusual type, namely AW 113/1928, with a vertical boiler, which carried the name (or logo) *Blaxters Ltd*. It was built by manufacturers Atkinson-Walker at Preston as one of just 25 engines built there between 1926 and 1931.

Beamish Museum Collection

sleepers, rails, wagons, a steam locomotive, rail ramps, points and crossings and a 'carriage'. The standard gauge locomotive was of an uncommon type, being a 4-wheeled vertical-boilered machine with geared transmission. It was obtained new from Atkinson-Walker (Works No. 113/1928). Fortunately a photograph of the locomotive has survived.

By the end of 1929 Blaxters had purchased some more, unspecified, items for their railway (costing just over £21) but they had allowed for depreciation on their equipment which was now valued at just over £813.

In 1931 they moved their head office to Slitrig Crescent in Hawick. The depreciation values allowed for their railway equipment were fixed at this time as 4 per cent per annum for their locomotive and 20 per cent for all other items. Thus, by 1935 the locomotive was valued at £583 and the rest of the railway at £172 17s. 0d. It is unfortunate that no sufficiently detailed surveys were conducted at this time and the track layout within the quarry appears to have been unrecorded. A stony track still followed the line of the former tramway, whilst the new main road access to the quarry was from the east.

Early in World War II Blaxters temporarily ceased using the quarry and some of the plant was disposed of. In particular in 1940 the steam locomotive was moved to Glasgow passing into the ownership of the contractor, J.W. Leask. Initially this company leased the locomotive to the contractors Paulings for use during the construction of a Royal Ordnance Factory at Wrexham but then in June 1942 they sold it to the Tottenham and District Gas Company Limited of London. It went out of use by 1945 and was scrapped in about 1955.

The company had clearly not made a final decision to dispense with rail operations for in 1945 they placed advertisements for a (presumably standard gauge) steam or diesel locomotive with four coupled wheels. No records appear to survive of any locomotive being brought to Blaxter Quarry as a result of the advertisements. However, there was the continued use at the quarry of a rail-mounted crane for lifting blocks of stone. The final date of Blaxters' operations here appears not to have been recorded.

Subsequent visits to the area revealed that the locomotive shed was still extant at the quarry in the late 1960s whilst a 'JAP' hand crane, apparently the one used by Blaxters, survived at Knowesgate station until at least 1959.

There was intermittent further stone extraction from the quarry in the mid- and latter-part of the 20th century. Tarmac used the quarry for a period until about 1984, though for the last few of these years the company was cutting and dressing stone from elsewhere at the quarry. Later in the 1980s a company known as 'Natural Stone Quarries Ltd' was removing stone. By 2000 the quarry was operated by Dunhouse Quarry Ltd, of Darlington. Since 2005 the operator has been Northumberland Stone Ltd, based in Bishop Auckland, County Durham. The reserves of stone at Blaxter Quarry are described as 'good' with quarrying being available from a face of six metres width beneath three metres of overburden. No rail systems have been employed recently, all stone being removed using road vehicles.

Blaxter Quarry is just 500 metres along a trackway from the main A696 road. However, this is private land and the quarry can only be visited with permission.

Chapter Nine

Proposed but not built
Railways and Cableways

Searches through documents held at record offices and in newspaper archives have revealed several descriptions and plans relating to mineral railways, cableways and tramways to transport stone which were proposed but, apparently, never constructed. In some cases rolling stock may have been purchased or moved to the site, or some rails may have been laid. Some of these railways were described in Volume One of this series. For several the carriage of stone was simply part of the proposals. The following lines were all proposed purely for stone movement.

26 - The Budle New Town Quarry Railway

A surviving 1828 'memo book' belonging to the quarry's then lessee, John Dodds of Alnwick, relates to the 'Budle New Town Quarry' (now called 'Brada Quarry') and proposals to construct a railway to allow the stone to be carried to Budle Quay, from whence it would be 'exported' by sea-going vessels. The ultimate destinations for the stone were to be Surrey and Kent where it was to be used in road-building. Delivery of the stone was to be at Surrey Coal Wharfs [sic] or Deptford Creek for ultimate use, for example, on the building of turnpike roads at New Cross and Woolwich, including the Dartford Road and Farnborough Road.

In that year it was proposed that an engineer should examine the 'Quay and Harbour' at the side of Budle Bay and survey the best route for a 'railroad', estimating its likely cost. Also to be investigated were the costs of an 'engine' to saw, break and lift stone, and a 'small steam boat with tug' for carrying 120 tons

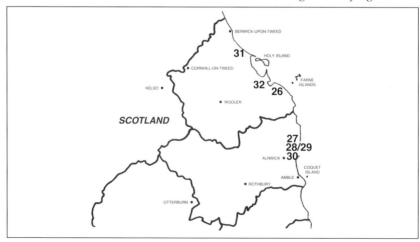

of stone. In addition the enlargement of the quay and improvement of the 'harbour' at Budle Bay were to be considered. Advice on the best size of hammer for breaking stones was also sought. Other contemporary correspondence related to the negotiations of a lease for the quarry, in particular a possible 'certain rent' of £500 for the removal of 8,000 tons of stone.

A report dated 11th December, 1828, was sent to Earl Grey, the local landowner, by Dodds. This report referred to the quantity of stone available at the quarry to be 'abundant' and the quality to be 'good'. The cost of starting operations at the quarry would be £2,145. Subsequent cartage costs would be 3*d.* per ton to 'the river' (referring to the Waren stream which flows into and through Budle Bay in a channel). It was proposed that a 'barracks' should be constructed for the quarrymen and labourers at the quarry. If a railroad were to be constructed then it would be better to weigh the stone at the quarry, in which case a weighing machine for the quarry would be needed. The section of the report on the existing jetty indicated that it was too small to cope with both the existing grain traffic and the proposed stone traffic. It was considered that without a railroad it would be necessary to allocate an area by the quay for the breaking, screening, weighing and shipping of the stone. It was recognized that there would be some problems in getting ships to call at the quay. Any associated plans and specifications relating to this report appear not to have survived.

The quarry was clearly brought into operation at the time for by 1829 there are references to a Mr White having been engaged as 'quarryman' and payments being made to quarry labourers and stone breakers working in the quarry. There was a sheerlegs crane working at the quarry and also a 'pump'. David Gibson, the grocer, saddler and ironmonger of Belford, had supplied powder and other materials to the quarry.

Furthermore, some stone must have been transported to its Surrey destination as on the 13th March, 1830 it was reported that a consignment of stones from 'Port Waren' to 'Surrey New Roads' had been both contaminated with dirt and deficient in measurement. However, the rest of the story of this enterprise is likely to remain undescribed as further documentation appears to be lacking. However, it is certain, from the absence of on-the-ground or cartographic evidence, that the railway was not constructed. This early 19th century shipping of stone probably did not last for long, as in 1911 even the most elderly residents of Bamburgh and Budle could barely remember the jetty being in use, and then their memories related to the grain trade, rather than that of stone.

27 - The Low Newton Quarry Tramway

A small quarry exists at Low Newton on the Northumberland coast (NU239248) which was operated, at the start of the 20th century, by a certain Edward Gibson, who paid £20 per annum to the landowner for the privilege of quarrying small quantities of stone. The entrance to the quarry is directly opposite the small mission church on the road leading to Low Newton

This former mine tub acts as a house name board at the end of the drive which leads past the former Low Newton Quarry. Former quarry lessee Mark Appleby is known to have moved both rails and tubs to this quarry in the second decade of the 20th century, though there is no suggestion that this is one of his tubs!   *Author*

A more modern mine tub is used to house a floral display outside a house, near to the National Trust car park, at Newton Links on the north side of Newton village. There was no quarry at this point though stone for local houses and walls was quarried elsewhere in the village.   *Author*

Seahouses. Gibson's lease empowered him to use railways or tramways but in view of the size of the quarry it is unlikely that he employed either of these, the stone being removed directly using horse-drawn carts.

The owner of the quarry in question was Mr Bolton Meredith Eyres Mansell, of Dumbleton Hall in Gloucestershire. In 1909, with Gibson's lease having expired, Mark Appleby, with successful quarry interests at Embleton and elsewhere, negotiated a lease for the extraction of whinstone and freestone. The lease was to have commenced on 11th November, 1909 and to have lasted 21 years. The fee to be paid for quarrying the stone was to be 1s. per cubic yard subject to a minimum annual payment of £20. Once again the lease specified that tramways or railways could be used to facilitate the movement of the stone.

In the event it appears that Mansell died for the lease which actually came into effect was effective between Mrs Caroline Sybil Eyres Mansell and Appleby. The lease was now to start from 14th March, 1910 and to last for the same period of 21 years. The same financial considerations as in the previously drawn-up lease were to apply, until 11th November, 1912 when an additional surface rent of £25 per annum would be applied.

As at Craster (*see later*), Appleby moved in his machinery and plant, including tubs, to the site ready for the start of work though, in practice, little stone seems to have been quarried here. Work had certainly finished by the end of the decade and in August 1920 some of the plant was sold from the site, a pump and boiler being sold, for example, on 6th August, 1920.

Further written documentation is lacking but subsequent Ordnance Survey maps have marked the quarry as 'Disused' or 'Old Quarry'. It is not known when Appleby finally vacated this quarry.

The present owners of nearby Quarry House have purchased a small four-wheeled mine or quarry tub which is plinthed at the end of the quarry lane and used as an attractive house name board, being planted with flowering plants. (Two larger and more modern mine tubs are located (2009) at the end of the driveway of Newton Link House and near to the entrance to the public car park at Newton Links, a short distance to the north at NU235261. These tubs also house floral displays in summer.)

28 - Mark Appleby's Quarry Railway at Craster

McLaren and Prowde were not the only local stone quarry operators to have an interest in obtaining Craster stone. In early 1910 Mark Appleby, who was operating quarries at Embleton and later at Belford, obtained a lease from the trustees of the will of the late Samuel Ayres, to develop a quarry at Norwell Brow and Hares Nick to the north side of the road as it approaches Craster village, that is, on the opposite side of the road from the quarries of McLaren and Prowde. The lease, actually dated 2nd May, 1910, allowed Appleby to quarry for 21 years from 11th November, 1909. He was to pay a royalty of 1s. per cubic yard of stone quarried, plus a surface rent of £15 per annum. Overall this would come to £50 per annum. The total area allowed for quarrying was 7½ acres. Appleby was allowed, under the terms of the lease, to construct such railways, tramways or roadways as he would require to take his stone to the harbour at Craster. There was a requirement that these, and the quarry, should be fenced. He was required to come to an agreement with the other quarry operators at Craster before the commencement of quarrying, presumably as regards the sharing of the shipping facilities at the harbour.

Appleby proposed a tramway from the quarry to the harbour (referred to as a 'dock') which would need to be '600 yards in length'. In addition there would be a need for some 200 yards of additional siding space. The line would be laid with 25 lb. rails to a gauge of 2 ft 6 in. The cost of this would be some £200. A self-acting incline, with the descending loaded wagons hauling up the empties was considered impossible on the grounds of an insufficient gradient. To operate the line, Appleby considered the use of either a steam engine (he had been using these on his line between Embleton and Christon Bank) or a steam winding engine. The latter was considered preferable as its boiler could operate other plant and tools within the quarry. The question of housing for the quarrymen was considered. The provision of sufficient cottages was estimated to cost £3,000, which, added to the cost of the tramway and various sundry costs, would mean an expenditure of £3,500 before the quarrying could commence. To repay this within 10 years it would be necessary to extract 42,000 tons annually for the first 10 years, to produce the necessary revenue of £350 per year.

The amount of stone quarried here by Appleby seems not to have been recorded though early on he certainly moved plant and machinery to the site, including a portable engine, a stone crusher (purchased from Ord & Maddison of Darlington) and a steam crane. Some rails were laid in the quarry but apparently not to the harbour as planned. An edition of the 1912 *Stone Trades Journal* referred to Appleby's quarried stone being transported to the harbour by cart:

> At Craster the stone has, so far, been conveyed to the coast by carts … and the harbour at present … [is] … most suited to cart traffic, but as it is developed, other means, such as a tramway or ropeway, would be used. The crushing plant is driven by a large portable steam engine at present. Underneath the whinstone quarry at Craster is an excellent freestone (sandstone), which is being worked and much used for local building work, and is a splendid weather stone.

However, it would appear that Appleby suffered the same downturn in trade as McLaren and Prowde, for in 1914, he was advertising the crane and portable engine for sale. One of the two cranes he sold in 1917 (for £43 11s. 0d.) was probably the Craster one. In April 1917 he removed the crusher to his newly-opened quarry at Belford. Then in May 1920 he sold the elevator and frame from Craster and in January 1921 the quarry's haulage gear. The rails within the quarry were presumably lifted and sold around this time, whether they were for scrap or reuse elsewhere is not recorded. There is no record of Appleby's proposed tramway to the harbour ever having been constructed. Subsequent editions of *Kelly's Directories* make no reference to Appleby's quarries here, Mark Appleby Ltd, being shown only 'of Embleton, Christon Bank and Belford'. However, Appleby must have continued to renew his Craster lease on several occasions because it was not finally surrendered until 1962.

29 - Lord Howick's Craster Railway and the Craster to Little Mill Aerial Ropeway

One puzzling document has come to light, in the form of a letter dated March 1910, which was addressed to local quarry lessee and stone dealer John Richardson. This refers to the planning by 'Lord Howick' of a whinstone quarry at Craster, with a tramway employing the full wagons to pull back the empties to the quarry (i.e. a gravity-worked self-acting incline). It was the intention to ship stone from the quarry, via Craster harbour, to Hull and the south. Whether this scheme was the same as that proposed for Appleby's quarry at Craster, described earlier, or was to be a separate enterprise, has not been discovered. If it were the same scheme as Appleby's it would seem very strange that Richardson, a potential competitor operating out of Little Mill Whinstone Quarry, should have been consulted or involved.

A separate letter exists in the Grey Archive, dated 21st November, 1919, from Mr T.W. Craster (of Craster) to the 5th Earl Grey concerning a proposal to construct a ropeway to carry stone from H.G. Prowde Ltd's quarry at Craster to Little Mill, to facilitate the transfer of stone to main line railway wagons at the sidings there. This ropeway (or aerial cableway) would have crossed the land of Earl Grey at a property called 'Windyside' near Little Mill station. Prowde was concerned about the viability of his operations at Craster and felt that without this connection to the main line rail system his operations would become uneconomic and have to cease. Mr Craster felt that it was preferable for any lease to be between himself and Earl Grey, but with the quarry operator, Prowde, paying the security of the rent for the ropeway. Earl Grey's letter of reply has not, apparently, survived. However, it would appear that he did not favour the proposal, for the scheme does not appear to have been taken forward. Such a scheme would probably not have found favour with John Richardson, still dispatching his own stone by rail from Little Mill.

Nothing 'on-the-ground' appears to have taken place as a result of either of these proposals.

30 - McLaren's Howick Scar Farm Quarry Tramway

In the 1920s McLaren, who had already had quarry interests at Craster proposed a new quarry to be opened at Howick Scar a short distance to the south. The site was to occupy 2.993 acres and would be located directly opposite a sea inlet known as 'Hole o' the Dike', south of Muckle Carr rocks. McLaren sought a 20-year lease and proposed to cart stone across Long Heugh and past Covert Plantation to the coastal road, though the indenture permitted the construction and use of tramways. A certain John Mansfield, working for the land agents George Grey & Sons of Milfield and Alnwick, wrote to James Cleghorn of the Howick Estates in cautionary terms. An attached note, clearly not for public viewing but referring to McLaren and his associates, read 'they are slippery fellows and want watching'! In particular the letter referred to some of the machinery in the existing Craster quarry as not having been paid for. It would appear that nothing became of this scheme to move the stone either by cart or by tramway.

31 - The Haggerston Estate Railway

On 7th February, 1901 a lease was drawn up between Mr C.J. Leyland, the owner of the Haggerston Castle Estate located to the south of Tweedmouth, and the representatives of a company to be known as Staen Ltd for the use of land to open one freestone quarry and three whinstone quarries at 'Beal', 'Black Heddon' and 'Fenham Hill'. The precise location of the first two has not been identified. However, one tiny quarry, believed to have been used for the manufacture of millstones, is located at Black Heddon in the Kyloe Hills, and another mid-19th century quarry is found to the east of the same hills on Buckton Moor. It is not known if either of these was the 'Black Heddon' quarry referred to in the lease. The quarry at Beal may have been the one located immediately to the east of the Beal station sidings, which was worked in the latter half of the 19th century. No 20th century quarrying appears to have taken place at these sites. Only Fenham Hill Quarry, of the three sites, can be positively located (NU073408).

Companies House have confirmed that Staen Ltd was incorporated in 1901 (Company No. 69695). The capital of the company was said to be £20,000 with Leyland owning half of the shares. As lessees, they were represented in their dealings by a Mr Gray, who requested, on their behalf, a period of one year to search for stone and then a 60-year lease. The agreed ground rent was to be £25 per annum with payments of 3d. per ton for freestone and 2d. per ton for whinstone. Rubble freestone was to be charged at 2d. per ton initially. The lease

In the early 1900s Messrs Staen Ltd proposed a railway from Fenham Hill Quarry to Beal station yard. The yard at this former station now forms part of a private garden with an impressive, cosmetically restored Peckett saddle tank, No. 1611 of 1923, as a 'garden feature'.   *Author*

was to permit the building of a railway to link the quarries with the main line at Beal, with the requirement that the line be securely fenced. The company decided that it was 'not only desirable but absolutely necessary in the interests of the promoters of the company … [that there is] … communication to the main line by a line of railway from the quarry'.

The company estimated that stone production would be around 12,400 tons per annum, with 10 quarrymen and three labourers being employed. They anticipated the carrying of manure, farm produce and 'like goods' over their railway, producing additional revenue of 2*d*. per ton! They expected that the North Eastern Railway would carry their stone from Beal to Berwick, the use of the NER's crane at Beal being available for the sum of 10*s*. per day. They were also contemplating using Kyloe Quarry, the stone to be brought from there to Beal by traction engine. They had approached the owners of 'loco traction engines' and a sum of 2*s*. per ton for transporting the stone had been agreed.

The company pressed on with its scheme: a steam crane was purchased for Fenham Hill Quarry and a crane was purchased for £10 from Christon Bank to be installed at Beal station. (This would have eliminated the need to pay fees for the use of the NER's own crane.) A payment of £9 11*s*. 10*d*. was made to the NER in July 1902 in connection with the Staen company's crane, with a further payment of £20 7*s*. 0*d*. being made in the following month. This was all reported to a company meeting.

However, things must have turned sour very quickly for the company because on 15th August, 1903 it was unanimously resolved by the Directors that it be wound up! Companies House record its present status as 'Dissolved', though no precise winding up date is indicated. No records of the quarrying of stone by this company have survived and it is most unlikely that any of the proposed quarry railway was ever constructed. Such a railway would have involved the construction of a cutting and a substantial inclined plane. No evidence of this exists on the ground and in aerial photographs of the area. The Fenham Hill quarry did, however, expand in size in the early years of the 20th century, though the stone was removed by road.

North Eastern Railway records, dating from some 10 years after Staen Ltd's demise, indicate that Beal Sidings were being used for the shipping of local stone, some 1,166 tons of roadstone being taken away in 1913, for example. Unfortunately the records do not indicate the quarry from which this stone was obtained.

At the time of writing Fenham Hill Quarry can be accessed from the lane linking Fenham Granary and the road below Fenhamhill (present-day spelling). This grassy lane is a public footpath forming part of St Cuthbert's Way but is also used for vehicular access to fields by the local farmer, making it very muddy on occasions. The quarry faces are largely obscured by vegetation though one exposed face reveals low quality friable stone towards its upper part with better quality stone below. The exit from the quarry is steep and it is most unlikely that a railway was constructed here. There is no obvious evidence of a loading bank in the quarry.

32 - *The Middleton Hall Quarry Railway*

The first record of the Middleton Estate supplying stone to the Northumberland County Council appears to date from 1910 when Colonel Leather sold whinstone for the improvement of the Alnwick to Eglingham road.

In 1920, the Surveyor's Department of the Northumberland County Council once again entered into discussions with Colonel Leather (who, by then, was ready to operate his own narrow gauge timber railway), for the opening of a stone quarry on the Middleton Estate for the production of roadstone. The precise location of the proposed quarry, planned to reach a maximum area of 5½ acres, was not referred to in the Minutes of the Council's Roads and Bridges Committee. However, it must have been towards the northern end of the estate as it was planned to transport the extracted stone by means of a narrow-gauge railway linking the quarry with Smeafield station (NU093380) on the North Eastern Railway's East Coast main line where a new exchange siding would have been needed near to the level crossing and its signal box. The line was to involve a level crossing over the A1 road. The council and Colonel Leather's representatives drew up an agreement for the lease of the quarry to extend for 21 years starting on 12th January, 1920. One locomotive would be required to operate the line and it would be necessary for a flagman to be provided at the A1 crossing. The quarry rent was to be £150 per annum with a premium of 6*d*. per ton of stone removed.

However, when consulted, Leather was not happy with the agreement and asked for further negotiations. An amended agreement was drawn up and dated 4th October, 1920. The lease was to start on 12th November, 1920 and last for 21 years with the same rental and stone premiums to be paid, but with some other details modified.

The county council proceeded to such an extent that, according to Minutes dated 3rd January, 1921, they had invited tenders for the supply of two engines to power the stone breakers in the quarry. Marshals had offered two for £356 10s. 0*d*. each. In addition by 12th February, 1921 they had purchased two Simplex locomotives at £741 each, one being required at Moor House Quarry near Alnwick, the other possibly for this line. The vendor's name is not recorded in the Minutes.

This lease did not result in stone being extracted from the Estate. Instead the County Council made the decision not to proceed with the use of this quarry and proposed railway, opting instead to use Hare Crag Quarry (q.v.), near Shilbottle on the Duke of Northumberland's Estate, for the quarrying of stone.

However, the county council had not finally given up the idea of obtaining stone from the Middleton Estate and in April 1930, following the closure of Moor House Quarry (q.v.) they sought to lease a certain Holborn Quarry from Colonel Leather and install quarrying plant. In June 1930 it was reported that an agreement with Leather could not be reached and the council's attention was switched to the possible use of quarries in the nearby Kyloe Hills, with direct loading of the stone into lorries at the quarry face. Even this scheme was not proceeded with, the county council continuing to obtain roadstone from its own quarry at Hare Crag, near Shilbottle.

Acknowledgements

I would like to acknowledge with much gratitude the assistance provided by the following 'official' organizations, individuals and companies that have been very patient and generous in responding to requests for assistance with my research:

Northumberland Record Office at Woodhorn (formerly at Gosforth and Morpeth), Berwick-on-Tweed Record Office (Linda Bankier and Carole Pringle), Durham Record Office, Tyne & Wear Archives Service, Somerset Record Office, Powys County Archives, Northumberland County Libraries at Berwick-upon-Tweed, Morpeth and Alnwick, City of Dundee Library, British Library (Map Library and Newspaper Library, Colindale), the National Archives at Kew, the Parliamentary Archive, Dundee City Archive, Tweeddale Press Group (*Berwick Advertiser*), *Northumberland Gazette*, *The Times*, Lloyds Register of Shipping, Berwick-upon-Tweed Civic Society, Berwick-upon-Tweed Preservation Trust (John Smithson), the Ordnance Survey, Durham Mining Museum, Industrial Railway Society (Dave Holroyde), Industrial Locomotive Society (Russell Wear and Allan C. Baker), the Historical Model Railway Society (Peter Swift), North of England Open Air Museum at Beamish, National Railway Museum Library, Companies House, Narrow Gauge Railway Society (Clive Walters), Henry Noon (Hunslet Engine Co.), the Ruston Archive (Ray Hooley), Devon Railway Centre, Fife Family History Society, Scottish Stone Liaison Group, Smiths Gore (James Boulton), Plateway Press, Forestry Commission (Kielder District), Australian War Memorial Research Centre, National Railway Museum (C.P. Atkins), Department of Veterans Affairs in Canberra, Australia (Richard Reid), Royal Artillery Museum (Matthew Buck and Paul Evans), Berwick-upon-Tweed Museum, Berwick-upon-Tweed Corporation (Freemen) Trustees, Wooler Information Centre, Glendale Gateway Trust, Northumberland County Council Conservation Team, Alan Keef Ltd, Northumberland National Park Authority, Northumbrian Water, Newcastle Local Studies Centre, Defence Estates, Ministry of Defence (Chris Livsey), Public Monument and Sculpture Association, Directorate of History and Heritage of the Canadian Department of National Defence, National Library of Canada and National Archives of Canada, Northumbria Rail, Aln Valley Railway Society (Vera Mallon, Gavin Head, Ken Middlemist and William Stafford), Road Roller Association, the Geological Society of London, British Geological Survey, Building Research Establishment, the Lagan Group, TARMAC Ltd, Hanson UK (David Weeks), Stirling Stone Group, LH Group Services (Henry Noon), Howick Estates, Northumberland Estates, Wallington Estates, Joicey Estates, Lilburn Estates Farming Partnership, Chillingham Castle (Sir Humphrey Wakefield), George F. White (Land Agents), Bailiffgate Museum in Alnwick (Gemma Taylor), the Thornycroft Register (Alan Sleight), Whitstable Museum (Craig Bowen), Railsearch Images (Thomas Carrick), The Irving Gallery, the Road Locomotive Society, the Royal Forestry Society, the National Trust (Harry Beamish), Leather Family Archives (Michael Greene), Belford Local History Society (Fiona Renner-Thompson), Taylor Wimpey, Bamburgh Golf Club (the late Gordon McKeag), Glasgow University Archive Services, Derbyshire Local Studies Library, and the Mitchell Library in Glasgow.

I have made use of the website of the Durham Mining Museum, the 'keystothepast' website of the Northumberland and Durham County Councils, and the 'Northumberland Communities' website of the Northumberland Archive Service. The website 'Access to Archives' (a2a) has been invaluable in enabling me to identify and locate a huge variety of documents. The internet, generally, has been a valuable research tool allowing me to access records, for example in Canada and Australia, which I would not otherwise have discovered. I have used census records available both on CD-ROM and on-line.

The records of the Industrial Railway Society, the Industrial Locomotive Society and the Narrow Gauge Railway Society (NGRS) have been invaluable in providing me with details of the various locomotives mentioned in the text. In return I have been pleased to pass on to them details which have not previously been in their records, or corrections arising out of my research. In particular I offer my grateful thanks to Dave Holroyde of the IRS and NGRS who kindly read through much of the manuscript, offered much helpful advice and corrected locomotive and other details.

In a recently published book on railways, an author apologized for not including the names of all of the '101 private individuals' who had provided assistance with his book. I would like to offer my grateful thanks to the 202 individuals (at least!) who have found the time to provide help during my eight years of research for this book. Your assistance, your letters, your emails and your telephone calls have been very much appreciated. Those who have offered photographs for the book will see their name appearing beneath those that have been used. If a photograph has not been used it may well have provided very useful information which I have incorporated into the book. If you have provided me with information, or directed me towards sources of information, I'm sure you will be pleased to recognise the relevant material in the text.

It is likely that there will be some errors or omissions. For these I accept full responsibility. I would be delighted to receive any photographs, corrections or additions which would make the descriptions of these minor railways more complete.

Every attempt has been made to identify the copyright owners of the illustrations used. However, some were obtained from unmarked photographic prints or old picture postcards purchased, for example, at postcard fairs. Often these have no means of identification and have thus been described as being from the 'author's collection'. My sincere apologies if your print has been used without permission.

Abbreviations for Locomotive Builders

AB	Andrew Barclay, Sons & Co. Ltd, Kilmarnock
FH	F.C. Hibberd & Co. Ltd, Park Royal, London
FJ	Fletcher Jennings & Co., Lowca Engine Works, Whitehaven
HC	Hudswell, Clarke & Co. Ltd, Leeds
HE	Hunslet Engine Co. Ltd, Leeds
HL	R. & W. Hawthorn, Leslie & Co. Ltd, Newcastle-upon-Tyne
Jung	Arn. Jung Lokomotivfabrik G.m.b.H., Jungenthal-an-der-Sieg
KS	Kerr, Stuart & Co. Ltd, Stoke-on-Trent
L	R. & A. Lister & Co. Ltd, Dursley, Gloucestershire
MR	Motor Rail Ltd, Simplex Works, Bedford
MW	Manning, Wardle & Co. Ltd, Boyne Works, Hunslet, Leeds
OK	Orenstein & Koppel AG, Berlin
RH	Ruston & Hornsby Ltd, Lincoln
S	Sentinel (Shrewsbury) Ltd, Battlefield, Shrewsbury
WB	W.G. Bagnall Ltd, Castle Engine Works, Stafford
Wcb	Whitcomb Locomotive Co., Rochelle, Illinois, USA

Bibliography

The following books and journals, in whole or in part, contain further reading or photographs related to some of the minor railways and industries in Northern Northumberland; all of these have been consulted.

The North British Railway in Northumberland by G.W.M. Sewell: Merlin Books
Main Line Railways of Northumberland by C.R. Warn: Frank Graham
Waggonways and Early Railways of Northumberland by C.R. Warn: Frank Graham
Rural Branch Lines of Northumberland by C.R. Warn: Frank Graham
Railways of the Northumberland Coalfield by C.R. Warn: Frank Graham
Industrial Railways in Northumberland and County Durham in the Days of Steam by Malcolm Castledine: Book Law Publications
A Regional History of the Railways of Great Britain: Volume IV The North East by Ken Hoole: David & Charles
Railway Stations of the North East by Ken Hoole: David & Charles
Forgotten Railways, North East England by Ken Hoole: David & Charles
Lindisfarne's Limestone Past by Roger C. Jermy: Northumberland Libraries
Lindisfarne Holy Island by Deidre O'Sullivan and Robert Young: English Heritage
Railways in Northumberland by Alan Young: Martin Bairstow Publishing
The Alnwick to Cornhill Railway 1887 to 1953 by Mary H. Brown: The Aln and Breamish Local History Society
The Alnwick and Cornhill Railway by John Addyman and John Mallon: North Eastern Railway Association
Industrial Locomotives of Northumberland: compiled by L.G. Charlton and Colin E. Mountford: Industrial Railway Society (a new edition, compiled and edited by Dave Holroyde, is in preparation)
Lost Railways of Northumberland by Robert Kinghorn: Countryside Books
Industrial Archaeology of North-East England (Volumes 1 & 2) by Frank Atkinson: David & Charles
Dam Builders' Railways from Durham's Dales to the Border by H.D. Bowtell: Plateway Press
The North Sunderland Railway by A. Wright: Oakwood Press
The Rothbury Branch by S.C. Jenkins: Oakwood Press
The Amble Branch by Bartle Rippon: Kestrel Railway Books
The Alnwick Branch by Bartle Rippon: Kestrel Railway Books
Border Country Branch Line Album by Neil Caplan: Ian Allan
Middleton, The Leathers and the Colonel's Railway by Tony Lee: Belford Local History Society
Memories of the LNER in Rural Northumberland by Allan Stobbs: published by the author
The Collieries of Northumberland Vol. 1 by James Tuck: Trade Union Printing Services
Longframlington: A look at the village through photos and stories by John West: published by the author
Wooler to Hexham and Return by Ken Veitch: The John Sinclair Railway Museum, Killingworth
Views of Wooler and Glendale by Derek Fairnington and Roger Mikel: MacLean Press, Wooler
Reflections, The Breamish Valley and Ingram by Sarah Wilson: Northern Heritage
We Can Mind The Time; Memories of Craster People: Ed. Colin Biott: Craster Community Development Trust
A History of Northumberland and Newcastle Upon Tyne by Leslie W. Hepple: Phillimore & Co.
Colliery Engineering: November 1930 Edition
Railway Bylines: various editions: Irwell Press
A Short History of Embleton Whinston Quarry; D. Malthouse; privately published monograph

Various newspapers have been consulted including copies of the *Berwick Advertiser*, the *Northumberland Gazette* and the *Cumberland News*, also trade journals including the *Stone Trade Journal, Contract Journal* and *Machinery Market*.

Bound volumes of the *Berwick Advertiser* are located in the offices of the company which still produces this newspaper in Berwick, though it is probably easier to conduct inspections at Berwick Public Library or at Berwick Record Office where most editions of this newspaper (and others covering the local area) are available on microfilm. It is advisable to book ahead to reserve a microfilm reader at both places.

Bound volumes of the *Northumberland Gazette* (and other early local newspapers which covered the Alnwick area) are held at the Bailiffgate Museum in Alnwick although they are not currently available for inspection. A few bound volumes, free to view, are kept at Alnwick Public Library. Other editions have been microfilmed and are available for inspection at the same library.

Microfilm copies of Berwick, Alnwick, Carlisle, Gateshead and Newcastle newspapers, also other journals, can be viewed at the Newspaper Library in Colindale, London, though it is essential to make reservations in advance.

The many original documents consulted can be found at various locations, including the Berwick-on-Tweed Record Office, the Northumberland Record Office at Woodhorn (formerly at Gosforth and Morpeth), the Durham University Archive, the National Archives at Kew, and in other public and private collections (see 'Acknowledgements'). Many of the colliery records, formerly with the Northumberland Record Office, have been moved recently to the North of England Institute of Mining and Mechanical Engineers in Westgate Road, Newcastle-upon-Tyne.

This 2011 photograph, taken at Budle Bay, shows how Brand's had improved the original grain jetty to facilitate the export of their stone. New facings of concrete were constructed and the original timber framework was filled in with rubble and concreted over. Two lines of rails were laid on the surface including one line of craneway for the two Thomas Smith & Son-built cranes. *Author*